THE OTHER SIDE

Finding Peace In The Middle of Your Storm

DUKE STONE

In memory of my dad, Dallas Stone. He taught me at an early age the value of servanthood and sacrifice. He and my mom have passed to the other side...where they are eternally in the presence of The Peace-Speaker

CONTENTS

FOREWORD

I have known Duke Stone for several years, and it is truly an honor to write the foreword for this book. From his very first project, it was clear that Duke is a gifted writer and story-teller. This book will also reach into your heart and challenge your soul with a longing to go deeper with our Savior.

His ability to draw the reader into each scene—placing you in the boat, in the storm, and in the tension of the moment—is exceptional. As I read, I found myself repeatedly thinking, "Get your highlighter out." *The Other Side* is filled with insight, truth, and spiritual gold nuggets. It is one you sit with, return to, and allow to shape you.

If you are ready to move beyond status quo living and into a faith that is active, obedient, and deeply trusting, this book is for you. While the account of Jesus and the disciples crossing the Sea of Galilee is familiar to many, Duke presents it with a fresh perspective that is both challenging and refreshing. This is not simply a story about a storm; it is an invitation to examine obedience, fear, trust, and trans-formation.

One line in particular captured my heart: *"Obedience becomes our yes to a journey we don't yet understand—faith that begins not with a blueprint, but with a command."* How often do we want clarity before commitment? Yet Jesus simply says, *"Let us go to the other side."* No explanation. No guarantees. Only an invitation to trust.

What I appreciate most about The Other Side is its honesty. It gives language to the questions we are often afraid to ask out loud—questions I know I have asked myself: Jesus, do You care? Do You see what's happening? Where are You, God, when the storm is raging? Rather than dismissing those questions or rushing past them, Duke invites us to sit with them and examine them in the light of Christ's authority and presence. Jesus may appear to be asleep in the storm, but He is never absent. And when He speaks, even the wind and the waves obey.

The Other Side is not only a powerful tool as an individual study guide, but is also well-suited for church-wide studies, leadership teams, and discipleship development. The ques-tions and practices throughout the book encourage honest heart inspection and meaningful conversation, making it a powerful tool for personal growth and transformation.

As you turn these pages, I hope that you will not simply stand on the shore, observing the journey, but accept the invi-tation yourself. Duke paints the promise of an exciting destiny for those willing to jump into the boat with both feet —choosing faith, trusting the command, and stepping into obedience.

It's an exhilarating faith leap to jump in the boat, but when you do, you will discover what God has prepared especially for you on *The Other Side*. But don't make this trip alone, go buy ten copies for friends and encourage them to journey to *The Other Side!*

Michelle Brooks-Young
Tennessee Church of God of Prophecy Outreach Coordinator
Former International Director of KidServe

HOW TO USE THIS BOOK

This book is designed to meet you wherever you are—whether you're in the middle of a storm right now, recovering from one, or preparing for the next storm. However you approach it, know that you're not alone on the journey.

———

FOR INDIVIDUAL READERS

If you are reading this book on your own, here is how to get the most from it:

READ THOUGHTFULLY: This isn't a book to rush through. Each chapter builds on the previous one, taking you deeper into the story of the storm and what it reveals about Jesus. Give yourself permission to slow down, to pause when something resonates, and to sit with truths that challenge you. Listen to the Holy Spirit's pace for you. There's no deadline. Some people will read one chapter per week. Others will need longer to process. The goal isn't to finish quickly; it's to be changed deeply.

ENGAGE WITH THE QUESTIONS: At the end of each chapter, you will find *Personal Exploration Questions* designed to help you apply what you have read to your own life. Don't skip these. Grab a journal or notebook and write out your responses. The questions are designed to move you from reflection to action, from insight to transformation.

COMPLETE THE PRACTICES: Most chapters include a *Practice* section with specific exercises to help you build spiritual strength. These are not optional add-ons. They are essential tools for growth. Set aside time to actually do them, not just read them.

———

FOR SMALL GROUPS

This book works beautifully as a group study. Here's how to make the most of it together:

RECOMMENDED FORMAT: 9-WEEK STUDY

- **Week 1:** Introduction
- **Weeks 2-9:** Chapters 1-8
- *Optional:* Add a 10th week for the Conclusion and final group discussion

SESSION STRUCTURE (60-90 MINUTES)
Opening (5-10 minutes)

- Brief prayer
- Quick check-in: "Where are you at right now— calm waters or stormy seas?"

Discussion (40-60 minutes)

- Invite someone to briefly summarize the chapter (2-3 minutes)
- Work through 3-5 of the Personal Exploration Questions
- Let conversation flow naturally—don't feel pressured to answer every question
- Focus on questions that resonate most with your group

Practice/Application (10-15 minutes)

- Review the Practice section together
- Let each person share which exercise they'll commit to this week
- Offer to partner with someone for accountability

Closing (5-10 minutes)

- Pray for specific needs that surfaced during the discussion
- Preview next week's chapter

GROUP LEADER TIPS

Create Safety. Some of these questions touch on deep pain, fear, and doubt. Establish ground rules early: what's shared in the group stays in the group, listen without trying to fix, and create space for honest wrestling.

You Don't Need All the Answers. Your role isn't to teach or correct. It's to facilitate conversation and point people back to Jesus. If a theological question arises that you can't answer, admit it and research together.

Manage Time Wisely. With 2-6 questions per chapter, you won't answer all of them. Before your session, select the 3-5 questions most relevant to your group. You can always suggest people journal responses to the others.

Encourage Practical Application. The Practice sections are where transformation happens. Don't let them become homework that people skip. Build in time for people to commit to specific actions and follow up the next week.

Be Flexible. If your group needs two weeks on a particularly heavy chapter (like Chapter 7 or 8), take it. The goal is depth, not speed.

FOR SPECIAL CONTEXTS

RECOVERY GROUPS If you are using this book in a recovery or support group context, Chapters 3 (Panic in the Boat), 7 (The Other Side), and 8 (The One Worth Everything) will be especially powerful. The theme of being "too far gone" confronts shame head-on with the truth of Jesus' relentless pursuit.

GRIEF/CRISIS COUNSELING This book speaks directly to those asking, "God, don't You care?" Chapters 3-6 walk through the progression from fear to faith in the middle of overwhelming circumstances. Consider pairing chapter readings with one-on-one or group counseling sessions.

MEN'S/WOMEN'S MINISTRIES The discussion questions work well for gender-specific groups. Each group may especially connect with themes that speak specifically to them.

A WORD ABOUT THE QUESTIONS

The *Personal Exploration Questions* at the end of each chapter are designed to:

- **Reflect:** Help you see your own story in the disciples' journey
- **Apply:** Move truth from your head to your life
- **Practice:** Build spiritual habits that anchor you in storms
- **Share:** Create opportunities for community and testimony

You don't have to answer every question. Choose the ones that resonate most. Let the Holy Spirit guide you to what you need most right now.

Some questions will be easy to answer. Others will sting. Some will make you want to skip ahead. Those are usually the ones you most need to ponder more deeply.

———

WHAT TO EXPECT

This book follows a clear arc:

CHAPTERS 1-2: The Setup You'll explore obedience, calm before chaos, and the reality that storms often come without warning.

CHAPTERS 3-5: The Crisis You'll walk through the disciples' panic, Jesus' rest, and the moment He speaks peace over the storm.

CHAPTER 6: The Transition You'll discover what happens when the storm ends and wonder begins.

CHAPTERS 7-8: The Purpose You'll see why the

storm mattered—the forgotten man waiting on the other side —and how Jesus' deliverance changes everything.

CONCLUSION: The Invitation You'll be invited to identify your own "other side" and decide whether you'll get in the boat with Jesus.

———

BEFORE YOU BEGIN

Take a moment right now to answer these questions:

Where are you in the storm?
- ☐ Calm waters (life is peaceful right now)
- ☐ Wind picking up (trouble is brewing)
- ☐ In the boat, fighting the waves (in crisis)
- ☐ On the other side, looking back (recovering/processing)

What do you hope happens through reading this book?

Write it down. Date it. At the end, come back and see how God answered.

———

A FINAL WORD

You picked up this book for a reason. Maybe you're in the middle of a storm right now, and you are desperate to know if Jesus really cares. Perhaps you are standing on a beach looking at someone everyone else has given up on. Or, are you that someone? Are you the one in the tombs, convinced you're too far gone?

Wherever you are, Jesus is already on His way to you. He has already decided you are worth the journey. The question is whether you will let Him reach you.

This book is about more than surviving storms. It's about discovering that the storm was never the point. The deliverance waiting on the other side is what really matters. The forgotten person Jesus crossed hell to reach is the heart of the story.

And here is the truth you will discover by the end: **You are that person.**

Jesus risked everything to get to you. The storm the disciples survived was the cost of your rescue. You are not forgotten. You are not too far gone. You are not the exception.

You are the reason He got in the boat.

INTRODUCTION

W E ALL HAVE SCENES FROM OUR CHILDHOOD ETCHED
indelibly in our minds. One of my most vivid memories
occurred in the spring when I was in third grade. It would be
one of those events that impacted the remainder of my life.

My family lived one-half block from Main Street, Coweta,
Oklahoma. No, that is not a euphemism for every small town
in the United States. It was the actual name of the street. The
three blocks of the street contained most of the small private
businesses along with a few chains like OTASCO (an acronym
for Oklahoma Tire and Supply Company) and Rexall Drugs
(yes, even our chain stores were regional). Our only fast-foods
were creatively named "Dairy King" and "Dairy Boy". The
only restaurant I remember was across the alley from our
home, "The Green Parrot Cafe".

That spring, my dad decided he had had enough of city
life and bought forty acres of pastureland in the countryside.
Well, I guess two miles from town was considered the country. As a few of the older male members of the family began

unloading furniture from our city house to our new-to-us country house, the April skies turned grey. After a brief rain shower and a small hailstorm, everything went eerily still. As we stepped outside, I saw it!

Tornadoes have been called "the finger of God" as they protrude from the overcast sky and make their way toward the ground. I had spotted the cyclone as it first began to develop and stretch toward the ground, about a mile to our southwest. We stood in awe for a few moments, then my dad yelled for all of us to get in the pick-up truck. Five of us crammed into the one-row cab, and my dad took off down the dirt road in front of our new home toward the paved road that would take us back to town.

As we made the right turn onto the paved road for the remaining mile into town, I remember looking over my shoulder to see the fully-extended funnel now dancing along the ground, still about a mile from us, moving perpendicular to the north from our position. I could see dust from the dirt road flying up over the small hill as we were speeding down the road. Then it happened.

My dad slowed down in front of a house on the road and started honking his pickup's horn frantically. Something he would do at the four or five houses on the road. He was warning them of the tornado approaching. My mind was screaming, "Are you crazy? We need to get out of here!" As an eight-year-old, I didn't know a lot about the safety rules when you have a tornado, but I figured being caught in a pickup truck with four other people wasn't high on the list of proper things to do.

Since you are reading this, you know that we survived, as did everyone else in our small town. In fact, the tornado was short-lived, dissipating before we even reached town.

I learned a lot about my dad that day. He wasn't highly educated. He'd left school in third grade to help support his family. But after I felt safe and could reflect on my father's actions, I knew that was the day he became my hero. He risked his safety and the safety of those who meant the most to him to warn his neighbors and friends.

———

FROM COWETA TO GALILEE

When I read the story of Jesus and His disciples who were caught in a storm on the Sea of Galilee, I'm reminded of that day in Oklahoma—a seemingly uncontrollable tempest, fear growing as the wind strengthened, and yet there was One calm presence in the middle of the chaos.

The disciples woke Jesus and cried, *"Teacher, don't You care that we're perishing?"*[1] It's an honest question, born from desperation. Haven't we all asked it at some point? "Jesus, do You even care?"

I know there have been seasons when my life darkened without warning: ministry storms, personal disappointments, prayers unanswered. Like those disciples, I have inwardly shouted, "Lord, do You even see what's happening?" Yet even in these moments, I've learned that Jesus may seem asleep, but He is never absent. His peace doesn't come from ignorance of the storm; it comes from authority over it.

Then came the moment that changed everything. Jesus stood, faced the chaos, and said, *"Peace, be still."*[2] The wind stopped. The sea calmed. Heaven spoke, and hell went silent.

This book explores what happens when our panic meets His presence, how the waves that threatened to sink us can become the place where He displays His power.

3

WHY I'M WRITING THIS BOOK

After years in ministry, I know this: storms are universal. Some are loud and public, others quiet and internal. All of them test what we believe about God.

> **After years in ministry, I know this: storms are universal. Some are loud and public, others quiet and internal. All of them test what we believe about God.**

This book is for those who are weary from rowing against the wind, who have cried out in the storm, who need to know, really know, that Jesus still commands the waves. It's for anyone who has wondered if peace will ever return.

Each chapter will take you deeper into that night on Galilee. From fear to faith, from trembling to trust, from storm to stillness. Until we reach the other side, where a surprise ending awaits.

WHAT YOU'LL DISCOVER

Like so many of the Bible stories we've known since childhood, what we often assume is the main point may not be the crux of what Jesus wants us to know. I think you will see that the heart of this story isn't in the storm that rages or even in the miracle that follows, but in the intricate details that are often overlooked.

By the time our journey with Jesus and the disciples is concluded, we may discover that the ultimate message is not in what happens to us during the storm, but in what Jesus intends to do through us once it's over.

The disciples began that night terrified. They ended it in awe, whispering, *"What manner of man is this, that even the wind and the sea obey Him?"*[3] God may not remove your storm, but He will redefine it. Before He calms your surroundings, He will calm your spirit.

––––––

SETTING SAIL

Like that day long ago in Oklahoma, when a funnel cloud descended and a quiet man risked everything to protect others, you may discover that true peace isn't found in the absence of danger. It's found in the presence of the One who commands the storm.

As the Apostle Paul faced his final days, he wrote, *"The time of my departure is at hand."*[4] The Greek word, *analýō*, means "to loosen" or "to set sail". It is the image of a sailor untying the ropes that hold a ship to the dock, setting it free toward its next destination.[5]

This is your moment of departure. Untie the lines that hold you to the familiar. The shore behind you is comfortable, predictable, and known. The horizon before you is where growth, revelation, and transformation await.

The Master has spoken: *"Let us go to the other side."*

Turn the page. The journey begins now.

––––––

REFLECT:

1. When have you experienced a "storm" that felt like it came out of nowhere? Describe that moment. What did it reveal about your faith, your fears, or your understanding of God?

2. The Oklahoma tornado story shows a father risking safety to warn others. Who in your life has modeled sacrificial love or courage during crisis? How did their example shape your understanding of God's character?

3. "Teacher, don't You care that we're perishing?" Have you ever prayed this question (even if you didn't say it out loud)? What prompted it? Looking back, how did God answer?

4. What "other side" might God be calling you to cross toward right now? What makes you hesitant to get in the boat?

CHAPTER 1

THE CALM BEFORE CHAOS

Obedience Often Precedes Opposition

"As evening came, Jesus said to his disciples, "Let's cross to the other side of the lake." (Mark 4:35)

———

THE DAY HAD BEEN LONG. THE KIND OF LONG THAT exhausts you. Crowds pressed in along the shoreline, hungry for every word Jesus spoke. Mark tells us that *"a great multitude"*[1] had gathered, and Jesus had given them truth in stories they could carry home.

He told them about a sower scattering seed on unpredictable soil. He spoke of a lamp meant for lighting, not hiding. He included a story about a seed growing silently beneath the surface, doing its work where no one could see. And then He painted a picture of a mustard seed, small enough to lose between your fingers, yet capable of growing into something sturdy enough to shelter birds.

Each story revealed another truth about the Kingdom. Each held a quiet invitation to trust what God can do with small beginnings and surrendered hearts.

As the sun slipped toward the horizon, the Galilean shoreline glowed with the deep reds and golds of evening. Jesus stood, dust on His feet, fatigue in His voice, and said to His disciples, *"Let us cross to the other side."*[2]

On the surface, it sounded simple. A boat ride. A break from the multitudes. A moment of quiet.

Some of them were fishermen after all. They were men who could read the sky like a scroll. In their world, there were no satellites, no Doppler radars, no "breaking weather alerts." Their forecasts came from observation, tradition, and the wisdom passed down by fathers and grandfathers.

Red sky at night, sailors' delight.
Red sky in morning, sailors' warning.

As they glanced upward, the sky was brilliant. A crimson color promised the sea would behave, the breeze would be kind, and the journey would be easy.

For once, obedience felt uncomplicated.

The Master spoke. They responded. No resistance. No confusion. No crowd demanding their attention.

They pushed the boat from shore, the cool water lapping softly against the hull. The strokes of the oars against the water and the quiet conversations among themselves were the only sounds in their quiet sanctuary. It was the kind of moment the disciples treasured. The rare calm where faith felt simple and following Jesus was uncomplicated.

Isn't that how obedience often begins? Clear direction. Calm waters. Those moments when we have a quiet confidence that we're exactly where we should be.

Faith, like the weather, can change without warning.

However, anyone who has followed Jesus for any length of time knows this: faith, like the weather, can change without warning. The skies can shift. The winds can rise. And the journey that began in peace can suddenly, violently turn into something that tests the deepest parts of us.

———

THE THREAD TO THE MIRACULOUS

There is a secret thread that runs through every extraordinary transformation in Scripture, a quiet ingredient that always accompanies the miraculous: obedience.

It never shines as brightly as faith. It seldom feels as thrilling as courage. But obedience is the hinge on which the ordinary swings open into the extraordinary.

Eugene Peterson captured this beautifully, "What we require is obedience—the strength to stand and the willingness to leap, and the sense to know when to do which."[3]

In a single sentence, he describes the tension woven into true discipleship: the long, steady endurance of a pilgrim and the sudden, breath-catching surrender of a worshiper who drops everything at God's command.

Scripture is full of people living in that tension.

When God told Abraham, *"Leave your native country, your relatives...and go to the land that I will show you,"*[4] Abraham packed his tent and left without a map. No GPS coordinates. No guarantee of safety. Just a command and a promise.

Centuries later, another man stood at another crossroads. Peter was weary from a night of failed fishing when Jesus, who was a carpenter, not a fisherman, said, *"Go out where it is deeper."*[5] Peter could have pushed back. He had the experience; Jesus had the audacity. His response reveals the heart behind every miracle of obedience: *"But if you say so...."*[6]

He let down the nets. And Jesus filled them. Both men learned what every disciple eventually discovers: obedience doesn't wait for clarity. Obedience creates clarity.

God's direction rarely arrives fully explained. His assignments seldom come with blueprints or guarantees. Every time we say "yes", whether whispered in weakness or declared in boldness, we open the door for the miraculous to enter our circumstances.

———

UNCOMFORTABLE WITH THE OTHER SIDE

The invitation didn't sound like much. *"Let us cross to the other side."* Eight simple words. But Jesus often wraps His most significant assignments in sentences that don't raise an eyebrow.

A story that has circulated on the internet illustrates this in a striking way. Robert was a tattooed biker who wore a leather vest and steel rings. He was the kind of man polite society tends to give space. He was picking up groceries one day when he saw an elderly woman fumbling in her purse, short on money and embarrassed by it. He felt a tug he didn't expect. Not a voice. Not a vision. Just a nudge to step in.

"Pay for her groceries."

It wasn't convenient. He wasn't the "random acts of kindness" type. But he obeyed the whisper, slid his card to the cashier, and offered to carry her bags. That act, so small he would have forgotten it by dinner, set off a chain reaction no one could have predicted.

Robert began visiting her, helping with chores, fixing what had broken, listening to stories no one else had time to hear. Grief from his own mother's lonely passing softened into purpose. Before long, his single act of obedience grew into a network of bikers across multiple states who checked on isolated seniors, repaired homes, provided rides, and restored dignity to people who thought the world had passed them by.[7]

One quiet yes became a doorway to hundreds of lives.

The disciples felt the same discomfort long before their boat touched the far shore. The *"other side"* wasn't simply a place on the map. It was the Decapolis, a cluster of ten Gentile cities filled with foreign customs and strange gods. Everything about it felt wrong. Unsafe. Unclean. Unwelcome. Their childhood warnings echoed with every splash against the hull.

Yet, that's where Jesus led them. Straight toward the place they would have avoided.

He wasn't just taking them somewhere. He was taking something out of them. Smallness. Suspicion. The quiet comfort of familiar faith. The boat ride was more than travel. It was spiritual surgery.

And He hasn't changed His methods.

Most of the time, His invitations come as interruptions. A

phone call we don't want to return, a problem we didn't antic-
ipate, or a responsibility we didn't ask for. Nothing about
these moments would be described as sacred. Despite the
discomfort of the moment, they become places where the
Spirit stretches us, surprises us, and sometimes confronts the
parts of ourselves we've managed to ignore.

Storms are loud, but a settled "yes" is louder. Waves can
shake you, but surrender will anchor you. And somewhere
beyond the horizon of your comfort, Jesus is already standing
on a shoreline you haven't seen yet, calling you not just to
cross over...but to become someone who can.

———

LET US GO TO THE OTHER SIDE

The word *us* in Jesus' invitation was no accident. It meant
they were not spectators. They were participants in a mission
bigger than their understanding. They were travelers, not
tourists. The *"other side"* was covered in spiritual darkness, a
region desperately in need of light. And Jesus wanted them in
the boat with Him.

He would carry the weight of the mission, but He invited
them into the work.

I'm reminded of one of my favorite photographs. My
then-four-year-old granddaughter, Isabella, was "helping" me
mulch the leaves with the lawn mower. We never drew up a
contract for "Papa and Bella's Mulching Service." It was
simply a spontaneous afternoon in the yard. If you had asked
her about her role, she would have announced with complete
confidence, "Me and Papa are mowing the yard!"

Of course, I was the one steering, guiding, and
preventing the mower from swallowing the shrubs. That

said, in her young mind, she was doing the heavy lifting. I loved her enthusiasm. I loved her sense of partnership. But more than anything, I loved that she wanted to do the work with me.

That is precisely how Jesus invites us to the other side. We may feel unqualified. We may feel overwhelmed. We may look at the need and feel hopelessly outmatched.

In those moments, two truths anchor the soul: First, He is in the boat with us. Second, He is the One who accomplishes the work.

As Paul writes, *"For God is working in you, giving you the desire and the power to do what pleases him."*[8]

Christine Caine captures this with striking simplicity: "Are you the answer to your prayers? I wonder how often, when we're praying and asking God to do something, He's waiting for someone to partner with Him to do it... God could solve every problem instantly if He chose to. But He's invited us to be His partners in bringing change to the world around us."[9]

When God calls you to the other side, He never calls casually. His commands carry destiny. We don't always see that destiny at first. He rarely reveals the obstacles in advance. He does not schedule a pre-trip meeting to explain the waves or preview the storm. He simply speaks.

Obedience becomes our "yes" to a journey we don't yet understand—faith that begins not with a blueprint, but with a command.

That evening on the Sea of Galilee, Jesus didn't give His disciples a detailed itinerary. He didn't outline what they would face. He didn't mention the violence in the wind or the panic that would grip their hearts. He simply said, *"Let us go to the other side."*

Most of the time, that is all heaven offers. One clear whisper: It's time to cross.

And the test becomes painfully simple: Will we trust His word enough to step into the boat?

———

A QUIET START

The disciples must have felt like they were on a vacation the first few minutes of the journey. After a full day of ministering to the crowd, passing out bread, answering questions, and managing needs, they were tired in the way only service can make you. The sea offered silence. No voices pressed in. No hands tugged on their sleeves. Just the hush of water and the soft glow of an evening sky that promised rest.

If they ever needed a quiet crossing, this was it. What they didn't know was how quickly calm would turn.

In the ancient Jewish imagination, the sea was more than a stretch of water. It symbolized untamed, unpredictable, and threatening chaos. The Hebrew word *tehōm*, used in Genesis 1:2 to describe "the deep," reflected those dark, unruly waters before God spoke creation into order.[10] That imagery followed Israel through the centuries. The sea represented everything uncertain, everything beyond human control. That is why the psalmist prayed, *"You rule the oceans. You subdue their storm-tossed waves."*[11]

For fishermen like Peter and Andrew, calm seas weren't just pleasant. They felt like Divine approval. And now Jesus was leading them straight into waters that would soon appear anything but.

It's easy to feel confident when obedience costs little and the seas behave. When everything is unfolding according to our plans, we assume the still waters confirm God's pleasure. However, as William Branham once observed, "The cloudy skies and storms of life are no signs of God's disapproval. Neither are bright skies and still waters signs of His approval."[12]

Anyone who has followed Jesus for long knows that calm seasons are often the warm-up for deeper tests. Faith feels effortless when it hasn't been challenged. God, in His wisdom, allows seasons of quiet to prepare us for seasons of stretching.

James wrote it plainly: *"When troubles of any kind come your way, consider it an opportunity for great joy... For you know that when your faith is tested, your endurance has a chance to grow."*[13]

That's why we must treat calm seasons with reverence. They are not confirmation that we got it right. They are preparations for the strength we will need later. The peace we feel at the beginning of obedience is not always meant to last. It is God's way of settling our hearts before the winds pick up.

We must treat calm seasons with reverence. They are not confirmation that we got it right. They are preparations for the strength we will need later.

"God created you fully knowing the moments that would cause you to question His faithfulness... He's allowed things in your life that have now created storms, disruptions, and even devastation."[14]

God is not absent in the storm. *"He displays his power in the whirlwind and the storm. The billowing clouds are the dust beneath his feet."*[15] Storm clouds are not evidence of God's distance. They are often the earliest signs that He is drawing near.

Maybe that's where you find yourself right now. The path looked clear when you started. You stepped out with confidence, but now the winds are shifting, and the waves are climbing. Your heart is tightening with questions you never expected to ask: Did I miss God? Did I misunderstand the assignment? Did I step out too soon?

Let me encourage you. Don't panic. The storm doesn't necessarily mean you have failed. The presence of wind doesn't always mean you have drifted off course. This is simply the part of faith where trust starts to cost something.

And always remember... **You. Are. Not. Alone. In. The. Boat.**

Faith doesn't begin in the storm. It is revealed there. The disciples didn't discover faith when the winds began to roar. Faith had already been planted in the stillness of the calm waters where trust was quietly taking root long before the sky turned dark. Their peaceful beginning was not a coincidence. It was preparation. They needed a memory of quiet confidence to return to when fear would soon scream louder than their hope.

God often works that way with us. He lets us taste His goodness, His nearness, and His peace first so that when the winds rise, we have something to hold on to. A reference point. A reminder. A memory of His faithfulness that steadies us when everything else begins to shake.

Faith isn't built in the chaos. It's forged in the quiet, when His presence feels near, when His voice feels gentle, when life gives you space to breathe. The calm before the storm isn't wasted time. It's a rehearsal. Practice. Spiritual conditioning.

You see, storms don't create faith, they expose it. They reveal what has been developing beneath the surface all along.

Storms don't create faith, they expose it.

So when life grows unusually quiet, resist the urge to grow restless. Savor the stillness. These are the sacred moments God uses to anchor your soul for the winds that lie ahead. During the calm, record moments He has proven Himself faithful to you. Memorize a couple of verses that remind you of His presence. Develop a rhythm of worship, even if it is just a few songs, so that in the turmoil, you can calm your spirit with the reminders of His greatness.

And when the storm comes, and it eventually will, you'll discover that the peace He planted in you during the calm has been preparing you to stand.

———

TAKING JESUS AS HE IS

There's a detail in Mark's account of their journey to the other side that often goes unnoticed: *"They took Him along in the boat, as He was."*[16] When Jesus said, *"Let's go to the other shore,"* they simply got in the boat with Jesus and began rowing. No adjustments. No negotiations. No second thoughts or extra planning.

And most importantly, they did not try to conform Jesus to their notions of what the command meant. They simply made room for His presence.

When we invite Jesus into our lives, we don't receive a modified version of Him, trimmed to fit our schedules or softened to accommodate our comfort zones. We receive the real Jesus—the One who sometimes sleeps through storms, who speaks truth that offends our pride, who leads us into deeper waters for the sake of growth.

We don't shape Him. He shapes us. Taking Jesus as our Savior means we surrender the illusion that we can manage Him. It means that we release our grip on how the journey should unfold and let His authority override our preferences, especially when His voice unsettles us.

Mary, the young Hebrew girl visited by an angel, under-stood this better than most. She had her own dreams: wedding plans, future children, simple hopes for a quiet life. But when heaven interrupted her story, she embraced God's plan over her own.

As Chris Tiegreen writes: "Mary had the privilege of receiving an announcement that God would rearrange her life... To be chosen for God's purposes means giving up our own."[17]

Mary didn't ask for assurances. She didn't demand clarity. She opened her hands and said, *"I am the Lord's servant. May everything you have said about me come true.*"[18] That is what it means to take Jesus as He is.

His presence is not seasonal or situational. It is continual. He comes into the workday and the dinner table, the late-night worries and quiet disappointments. When He steps into our boat, even though the waves may still crash, fear loses its grip.

Because once He's in your boat, the destination is secure, even when the route gets rough. His presence doesn't promise a smooth voyage, but it guarantees a safe arrival. You may not know what waits on the other side, but you can trust the One who said, *"Let us go to the other side."*

———

The disciples were settled in for a peaceful evening resting on the Sea of Galilee. They were unaware that the serenity of the evening would soon erupt into a storm that would challenge everything they believed.

What began as an act of obedience would soon become a battlefield of wind and waves, revealing the power of the One they followed and the truth about their own faith. The lesson of the calm had been received. Now, the lesson of the storm was about to begin.

———

REFLECT:

1. **Obedience often precedes opposition."** Think of a time when you obeyed God and immediately faced unexpected resistance. How did you interpret

that resistance? Did you question whether you'd heard God correctly?

2. **The disciples began their journey with clear skies and calm seas.** Describe a season when following Jesus felt easy and uncomplicated. What did that calm season prepare you for that you didn't realize at the time?

3. **Eugene Peterson wrote about "the strength to stand and the willingness to leap, and the sense to know when to do which."** Which do you find harder—standing firm when nothing seems to be happening, or leaping forward when God calls you into something uncomfortable? Why?

4. **"Taking Jesus as He is" means surrendering control of how your journey unfolds.** What aspect of your life are you most tempted to keep in your own hands rather than fully surrendering to Jesus?

5. **The chapter mentions developing spiritual conditioning during calm seasons.** What spiritual practices help you build strength during peaceful times? Are you currently investing in those practices, or waiting for the next storm to force you back to them?

Practice
Build Your "Faith Anchor" Before the Storm. Calm seasons are preparation grounds. Use this time to build spiritual strength before the next wave rises. This week, complete these three exercises:

1. **Document God's Faithfulness.** Write down 3 specific times God proved Himself faithful to you:

   - What was the situation?
   - What did you fear would happen?
   - How did God show up?

Keep this list accessible (phone notes, Bible, journal). When the next storm hits, read it before you panic. This is your evidence that God doesn't abandon you.

2. **Memorize Your "Let Us Go" Verse.** Choose one Scripture to anchor you when God calls you into uncomfortable territory. Write it on a card. Read it aloud daily for one week. When God says, "Let us go." into your storm, this verse will be ready.

   - Joshua 1:9 - "Be strong and courageous… for the LORD your God is with you"
   - Philippians 4:13 - "I can do all things through Christ who strengthens me"
   - Isaiah 41:10 - "Fear not, for I am with you"
   - Proverbs 3:5-6 - "Trust in the LORD with all your heart"

3. **Practice One Small Act of Obedience.** Faith muscles grow through use. Don't wait for dramatic callings—practice obedience in small things now. When you obey in small things during calm seasons, you build the spiritual muscle memory to

obey in big things during storms. The calm isn't wasted time—it's training time.

This week, do one thing God has been nudging you about:

- Have the conversation you've been avoiding
- Send the apology text
- Give the generous gift
- Serve in the way you've been resisting

Write down:

A. What I will do: _____
B. When I will do it: _____
C. What happened when I obeyed: _____

CHAPTER 2
WHEN THE SKY TURNS BLACK

Storms Often Arise Without Warning, But Never Without Purpose

And there arose a great storm of wind, and the waves beat into the ship, so that it was now full." (Mark 4:37 KJV)

———

IT WAS SUPPOSED TO BE A PERFECT DAY ON LAKE TAHOE.

The kind of day that makes you breathe a little deeper. Sunlight sparkled on the water. The lake shimmered blue, and it was quiet, framed by mountains still carrying a little winter on their peaks. Ten friends climbed into a 27-foot Chris-Craft to enjoy the kind of afternoon you remember later and smile about.

No one expected trouble. Then again, storms don't always come with warnings.

A light breeze picked up. Nothing unusual. Then the temperature dipped. The wind shifted. And in less time than it takes to finish a conversation, the lake changed its mood. The sky dimmed. Waves rose higher and harder. The wind howled down the basin at a speed no one on that boat had prepared for. Before they could make sense of it, eight-foot swells slammed the vessel broadside, flipping it and throwing everyone into the icy water.

Rescue teams rushed out as fast as they could, but they were fighting the same fury. By the time the storm spent itself out, six were dead and two were missing.[1]

In moments, joy had turned into terror.

Meteorologists later called it a microburst, a term for something wild enough that it can undo a day and end a life. However, anyone who has ever been blindsided by trouble doesn't need a definition. You know how it feels.

One breath, you're steady. The next, you're thrown into waters you never prepared for.

That's exactly where the disciples found themselves that night on the Sea of Galilee. These men weren't amateurs. Some had fished that lake since childhood. They knew how to read its nuances and temperament. So when Jesus said, *"Let's cross to the other side,"* they didn't blink. The evening was quiet, the air cool, the sky beginning to glow with early stars. Everything about the moment suggested peace.

Then it happened.

A gust that didn't belong there. A burst of wind that made every fisherman's instincts turn sharp. In seconds, the calm surface churned. Waves slammed against the boat. Water spilled over the sides faster than they could throw it out. The roar of the storm swallowed their prayers. What had been a gentle crossing earlier that evening became a desperate fight to stay alive.

That's the thing about storms. They don't wait for a convenient time. They show up uninvited. They arrive fast and they hit hard.

That's the thing about storms. They don't wait for a convenient time. They show up uninvited. They arrive fast and they hit hard.

Both storms, the one on Tahoe and the one on Galilee, remind us how quickly life can change. One phone call. One diagnosis. One text message that stops you cold. Moments earlier, you felt safe. Then suddenly you're gripping something solid to stabilize yourself because everything familiar is shaking.

Here's the truth beneath both stories: the storm didn't catch Heaven by surprise.

What knocks the breath out of us never rattles the One who commands the wind. What we never saw coming is already under His authority. The same Jesus who sent the disciples onto that lake is Lord over the storm that rose upon it.

Sometimes it takes a dark sky to show us just how bright His peace really is.

―――

WHEN STORMS STRIKE SUDDENLY

The hills surrounding the Sea of Galilee form a natural wind tunnel, where chilly mountain air rushes down and collides with the warm currents rising from the lake. It's a recipe for a perfect storm: sudden, fierce, and frightening.

That night, the disciples experienced one of those moments. The text says, *"There arose a great storm of wind."*[2] There were no warning signs, no dark clouds forming on the horizon, no shift in the smell of the air. Just a gust, then another, until the sea turned violent beneath them.

That's how storms come, isn't it? You can be doing everything right, following Jesus faithfully, when suddenly the wind shifts. Without notice, your calm becomes chaos. The diagnosis comes. Friendships fracture. Your finances collapse. What began as an ordinary day on familiar water turns into a night you'll never forget.

Mark's description tells us something deeper. He uses a striking phrase: *"breaking into."*[3] The Greek word is *epiballō,* and it's rarely used for weather. In the ancient world, this word described people throwing something at someone else— a deliberate act, a targeted force.[4] Out of the nineteen times it appears in the New Testament, this is the only time it describes the weather.

This storm wasn't just strong. It felt personal.

The disciples were not in the storm because they were out of God's will. They were in the storm because they were right in the center of His will. Jesus told them to get into the boat, and their obedience had placed them on the lake. That's what makes some storms so confus*ing*. When the journey begins with *"Let us go to the other side,"* it can lead straight into resistance you never expected.

Jesus had not misread the weather. He knew what was coming. He always does. Sometimes He sends us into storms not to punish us but to prepare us. Not to drown us but to deepen us. The same voice that said, *"Let us go,"* had already secured the outcome.

We want faith to mean safety. Yet, when we follow Jesus, faith often means obedience, even when the sky turns black. If He sent you, He will sustain you. What surprises us never surprises Him. He is never unprepared, never out of position, never asleep at the helm.

We want faith to mean safety. Yet, when we follow Jesus, faith often means obedience, even when the sky turns black.

Storms remind us that the faith we profess in calm waters must now anchor us in the tempest. Faith isn't proven by how you start the journey. It's revealed in how you respond when the sky turns black.

THE BATTLE BEHIND THE STORM

When you remember what waited on the other side of the lake, it's easy to see a sinister power working against them. On the other side was a tormented man crying out among the tombs and a region steeped in spiritual darkness. Everything about this storm carried the scent of resistance. It wasn't simply wind and water. It was pushback. Something bent on stopping Jesus before He ever reached the shore.

I don't blame Satan for every flat tire or headache I experience. I've heard people say, "Pray for me; the enemy is attacking my blood sugar." And while I never say it out loud, sometimes I want to reply, "That wasn't the enemy. That was the plate of brownies you polished off at midnight." Or, "Pray for my finances; the devil is fighting my bank account." Again, the thought crosses my mind: "Maybe it's not the devil. Maybe it's that credit card charging 29% interest."

We give the enemy too much credit for things that are simply the consequences of our choices. But don't let that swing you too far in the other direction.

We do have an adversary. One who has a very clear mission: *"to steal and kill and destroy."*[5] He does everything he can to intercept God's work in us and through us. And when you step toward God's will, you shouldn't be surprised when resistance rises.

It was no accident that this storm attacked the boat headed toward a demonized man who desperately needed freedom. The enemy had held that territory for a long time. If Jesus reached the shoreline, hell's grip would break. So the only option was to stop the boat before it ever arrived.

When Jesus said, *"Let us cross to the other side,"* He wasn't suggesting a pleasant evening sail. He was announcing a Kingdom advance into enemy-held territory. Mark Batterson captures Jesus' intention when he wrote: "Faithfulness is not holding the fort. It's storming the gates of hell and taking back enemy territory that belongs to God."[6]

That's precisely what this moment represented. Not retreat, but advance. The Enemy resists us because obedience advances the Kingdom. When you step out in faith, you're not just entering unfamiliar territory. You're entering contested territory. The storm that rose against Jesus and His disciples was hell's counteroffensive to a heavenly invasion.

Paul understood this dynamic when he wrote, *"A great and*

effectual door is opened unto me, and there are many adversaries."[7]
Opportunity and opposition always show up together.

The Devil cannot create. He can only corrupt. Only God is the Creator. Satan twists what already exists. The same wind that once carried the breath of God into Adam's lungs was now being manipulated by the *"prince of the power of the air."*[8] He uses what is natural to accomplish what is spiritual: confusion, fear, distraction, and paralysis. His aim is not simply to frighten you but to divert you.

That's precisely what he tried to do with the disciples. If he could turn their obedience into frustration and fear, he could derail their mission before they ever reached the other shore. For when you lose confidence in the One who sent you, you will abandon the course He set for you.

The disciples fought the waves with everything they had. They strained at the oars. They bailed water. They shouted instructions over the roar. They did what experienced fishermen do when a storm rises: they battled what they could see.

Yet, the real fight was in what they couldn't see.

While they wrestled with the waves, Jesus slept. He wasn't indifferent. He wasn't careless. He simply was not defined by the chaos that terrified them. He knew what they hadn't yet learned: if you silence the spiritual, the natural will fall into place.

The same holds true for us. You can't calm the storm around you while a storm rages inside you. You can't speak peace over your circumstances until you've let Christ speak peace into your soul.

> **You can't calm the storm around you while a storm rages inside you.**

Paul would later write, *"We wrestle not against flesh and blood, but against principalities, powers, and the rulers of darkness in this world, against spiritual wickedness in high places."*[9] The enemy's strategy hasn't changed. He disguises the battle, muddles the source, and nudges you to think it's nothing more than a coincidence.

Storms have a way of revealing the spiritual conflict behind what looks like an ordinary struggle. The battle wasn't only in the wind. It was in the disciples' minds. Fear whispered, "Maybe He doesn't care. Maybe he's forgotten you."

Yet somewhere beneath the roar of the wind and the crash of the waves, another sound was present. It was the quiet, even breathing of the One who slept. Jesus wasn't anxious. His peace didn't depend on calm seas. He rested in the certainty of His authority over everything, including the storm.

The storm may have been Satan's attempt to disrupt the journey, but it would become the stage for Jesus to display His power. That's the way God works. What the Enemy hurls to drown you becomes the very platform where God reveals His strength in you.

A MODERN STORM, A TIMELESS SAVIOR

That truth is not confined to a boat in the first century. It shows up in hospital rooms, in recovery centers, in moments when your body or your hopes feel like they're breaking apart. It showed up powerfully in the life of Katherine Wolf.

On April 21, 2008, Katherine was a 26-year-old mother with a six-month-old baby boy when a massive brainstem stroke nearly took her life. The doctors gave her husband, Jay, devastating odds. If she survived the surgery, she would likely never wake up. If she woke up, she would never be the same.

But Katherine did wake up. And the journey that followed was longer and harder than anything she could have imagined.

Eleven surgeries. Months of therapy. Learning to walk again. Learning to speak again. Watching her husband care for their son while she sat trapped in a body that wouldn't cooperate. Seven months into that journey, she sat in a wheelchair watching Jay play with their baby boy. Laughter filled the room, but despair filled her heart.

She wondered quietly, "Has God made a mistake?"

The storm felt too big. Her body felt too broken. Her world felt too far gone. Everything she had known—her independence, her future, her sense of purpose—had been stripped away in an instant. She had done nothing wrong. She had been faithful. And yet here she was, in the middle of a storm she never saw coming.

And then something happened. It wasn't loud and dramatic. It was a whisper, but it steadied her soul.

Katherine describes it as a deep awakening of God's Word rising within her: "Katherine, you are not a mistake. I DON'T MAKE MISTAKES. I know better than you know. I'm God, and you're not."

Truth cut through the storm like light breaking through cloud cover. Right there, in her pain, weakness, and waiting,

God met her. Hope didn't arrive in a dramatic rescue. It came in a whisper that reminded her who held her life and who held her future.

"It changed everything," she later wrote. "My body didn't work—but my soul was still alive with purpose."[10]

Katherine discovered what the disciples would soon learn. Storms do not get the final word. Jesus does.

Today, Katherine and Jay share their story around the world, encouraging others who are facing their own unthinkable storms. Her body still bears the marks of what she endured. But her faith bears witness to something deeper: God's presence in the storm is more powerful than the storm itself.

The same Jesus who spoke to the wind on Galilee spoke to Katherine in her hospital room. The same authority that calmed the sea calmed her soul. And the same hope that anchored the disciples in their darkest hour can anchor you in yours.

If the winds are rising in your life and your faith feels unsteady, let this truth settle deep in your soul. The storm isn't where your story ends. It's where His strength begins.

————

DISCERNING THE STORM YOU'RE FACING

Not every storm has a spiritual source, but when one does, natural wisdom fails and spiritual discernment must lead. The disciples saw only wind and waves. Jesus recognized the battle beneath the surface.

Every believer eventually has to learn how to recognize that dividing line. You can't fight a spiritual battle with natural weapons. And you won't out-think a spiritual assault with logic alone.

When a storm rises in your life, slow down long enough to listen. Ask the Lord three simple questions: Is this storm connected to a choice I made? Is it simply part of living in a broken world? Or is this resistance because I'm moving toward God's will?

Take a moment to write down what you sense. Discernment rarely comes in the noise. It comes in the quiet, steady spaces where your heart can hear Him. Once you recognize the source, you'll know how to respond: repent when the storm is self-inflicted, endure when the world has shifted beneath you, and stand firm when the resistance is spiritual.

Some storms require repentance. Others require endurance. And some require spiritual warfare. Clarity won't remove the storm, but it will give you the courage to face it.

———

THE TEST OF FAITH

The storm on the Sea of Galilee didn't just appear out of nowhere. It pushed against Jesus' mission and pressed hard on the disciples' confidence. The wind exposed more than the surface of the water; it exposed what was happening inside those men.

Their obedience had placed them on that lake, but the storm revealed whether they trusted the One who told them to go. They had watched Him heal the sick and teach with authority. They had heard His words and seen His heart, but storms have a way of asking a more difficult question: Will you believe Him when the world around you doesn't match what He said?

Spiritual battles aren't fought to determine who holds the greater power. That was settled at Calvary. They test whether we will trust what Christ has already secured.

So, when the wind picks up and darkness edges in, don't confuse it with abandonment. It may be the moment God is inviting you to witness His power again. *"No weapon formed against you shall prosper."*[11]

Storms may come, but they cannot stop what God has ordained.

———

The disciples didn't know it yet, but they were about to witness something that would change everything. The wind that threatened to drown them was about to meet the Word that created it. The waves that crashed against their boat were about to bow to the One who set their boundaries.

The storm was loud. Even so, the voice of Jesus would be louder.

In the chaos of that terrifying night, they were about to learn the most important lesson of all: the One who sleeps in the storm is the same One who commands it.

———

REFLECT:

1. **The Lake Tahoe tragedy reminds us that storms arise without warning.** What storm in your life caught you completely off guard? How did

the sudden shift affect your trust in God's goodness?

2. The Greek word *epiballō* suggests the storm felt personal and targeted. Have you ever felt like difficulties in your life weren't just random circumstances but spiritual resistance? How did that awareness change the way you responded?

3. **"Sometimes He sends us into storms not to punish us but to prepare us. Not to drown us but to deepen us."** Looking back at a difficult season, what did God prepare or deepen in you that wouldn't have developed any other way?

4. **Katherine Wolf's story shows how God met her in the middle of overwhelming loss.** When have you heard God's voice most clearly—in the calm or in the chaos? What did He say to you?

5. **The chapter challenges us to discern the source of our storms.** Take a moment to consider a current difficulty you're facing. Is this connected to a choice you made? Is it simply part of living in a broken world? Or is it resistance because you're moving toward God's will? How does identifying the source change your response?

PRACTICE:
Write down your "storm strategy" before the next difficulty arrives:

- **Spiritual action:** What will you do first when fear rises? (Example: "I will pray before I panic")
- **Relational action:** Who will you reach out to instead of isolating? (Name a specific person)

- **Practical action:** What decision-making boundary will you set? (Example: "I will not make major decisions until the crisis passes")

Place this strategy somewhere visible: inside your Bible, on your mirror, or as a note in your phone. When chaos hits, you'll already have a Christ-centered plan in place that steadies your mind and anchors your faith.

CHAPTER 3

PANIC IN THE BOAT

Fear magnifies the waves we were meant to walk through.

"Then he asked them, 'Why are you afraid? Do you still have no faith?'" (Mark 4:40)

———

IT HAPPENED FAST.

The night that began in quiet obedience came apart before they even realized what was happening. The soft wind stiffened. The waves rose. Water poured over the sides faster than their tired hands could toss it out. The boat rocked and groaned, every plank straining under the pressure of the storm.

Fear stepped in and took control.

Even the fishermen, the ones who knew the Sea of Galilee as well as they knew their own families, felt themselves losing the battle. They had seen storms in every season. They had survived sudden gusts that could rattle the shoreline. This one was different. It carried intention. It felt aimed at them.

And through it all, Jesus slept.

To the disciples, that made no sense. How could He rest while they were fighting to stay afloat? How could He remain so still while the wind swallowed their voices? Fear grew in their minds until it formed a single desperate question: "Teacher, don't You care that we're perishing?"

That is how fear works.

It twists what is true.

It turns prayers into accusations.

It takes our eyes off His promises and fixes them on whatever wave is rising next.

The disciples trusted what the storm told them more than what Jesus had already said. They did not understand that His rest was not indifference. His calmness was a quiet declaration of authority.

The peace within Him would soon speak to the chaos around them.

However, before that happened, Jesus would deal with something more dangerous than wind and water. Fear had begun to drown them long before the lake tried to.

Lee Eclov tells a story about the way fear confuses clear thinking. After the Battle of Gettysburg, thousands of rifles were collected from the field. Most were still loaded. Many had been stuffed with several charges, one stacked on another, because panicked soldiers kept reloading but never pulled the trigger. One rifle held twenty-three loads packed tight in the barrel. Fear had frozen them.[1]

This chapter enters that kind of moment. It is where faith hesitates and fear takes the lead. It is where our voices shake and our assumptions crumble. It is where the disciples speak words they never thought they would say. And if we listen closely, we will hear ourselves in their cry.

The storm was loud. Their fear was louder. Yet right there, in the middle of the chaos, Jesus was preparing to reveal that His greatest works do not always wait for calm seas. Sometimes they begin when a fragile faith rises again.

———

WHEN FEAR TAKES CONTROL

The storm came in waves. Not only across the sides of the boat, but across their confidence. Each gust pushed a fresh surge of water against the hull. Mark tells us that the waves were crashing into the boat, and the water was rising fast. The same men who once bragged about surviving Galilee's worst nights were now gripping the rigging with trembling hands. Panic sat in their throats. Faith was slipping through their fingers as quickly as the water they tried to throw back into the sea.

They began this journey convinced they were heading in the right direction. Jesus had said they were going to the other side, and that was enough. They climbed into the boat without a hint of resistance. Yet obedience did not shield them from hardship. It placed them, as it often places us, in its path. In the middle of that storm, the command that once felt clear now felt like a mistake.

Fear is like that. It steps forward and takes control when circumstances turn violent. Trusting Jesus on a quiet lake is one thing. Trusting Him when the waves feel taller than your faith is something else. Their boat was filling. Their courage was draining.

Fear has a way of making everything personal. It whispers that the danger is closing in on you alone. It turns good sense into reaction and reaction into retreat. Before long, fear is deciding your next step.

Fear has a way of making everything personal. It whispers that the danger is closing in on you alone.

Any boat filling with water is in danger. Any heart filling with fear faces a similar threat.

It does not take much to shake any of us. A doctor uses a word you never wanted to hear. A message ends a relationship. The economy shifts without warning. A phone call comes late in the night. In a moment, the heart can move from steady trust to a tidal surge of fear.

Fear does not always shout. Sometimes it arrives in a quiet sentence that slips across your mind. You might hear something like, "This is the moment you will not survive." Or, "God has forgotten you." Or, "You are carrying this alone." When fear gets hold of your heart, it begins rewriting the story. The disciples were convinced they were going to perish. Jesus had already told them they were going to the other side. The difference between the two stories depended on which voice controlled their thoughts.

In moments like these, faith does not vanish. It shifts. The disciples still believed, but they believed the wrong thing. They put more confidence in the strength of the storm than in the promise of Jesus. David once wrote, *"My heart pounds in my chest. Fear and trembling overwhelm me, and I cannot stop shak-*

ing."[2] Even so, God had not left him, and He had not left those trembling disciples. The storm never silenced the voice that called them on the journey. That voice was waiting for the moment when their desperation would drive them toward Him again.

———

THE ACCUSATION IN THEIR CRY

That's exactly what happened in the boat. Fear didn't just fill their hearts. It filled their mouths.

The wind kept rising. The waves kept reaching higher. Water pushed its way into the boat, and the men who walked with Jesus were convinced the end had come. If I had been there, I would have asked the same question they must have wondered in their hearts. Where is Jesus in all of this?

I know that because I have asked it in far smaller storms. I have felt the tension of frightening circumstances and whispered, "God, where are You?" And like the disciples, I did not always like what I saw. There have been moments when it felt as if He was resting somewhere far away while I was trying to stay above the waves.

The twelve men had been shouting instructions to survive the storm, but when their strength failed, they turned toward the only One who seemed untouched by the chaos. They shook Him awake and cried, *"Teacher, don't you care that we're going to drown?"*[3]

To them, His sleep felt like distance. Their fear came out as an accusation. Panic can often give words to what is hidden deep in the heart.

It is easy to look back and critique their reaction, but most of us have prayed something similar.

"Lord, don't You care that my child is hurting?"

"Don't You care that my life is slipping through my hands?"

"Don't You care that I am overwhelmed?"

Fear rarely stays quiet. It raises its voice. It fills the heart with questions that sound more like frustration than faith. Yet their words were not blasphemous. They were honest. Fear speaks honestly, even if the honesty is born from confusion. The danger beneath their words was not their desperation. It was the conclusion they were drawing. They mistook His stillness for a lack of concern.

They did not yet understand that His silence was not absence. His rest was not neglect. The storm would become the place where He revealed just how deeply He cared for them.

We often fall into the same trap. When heaven seems quiet and prayers echo back unanswered, we question God's compassion. We do not question His ability. Most of us believe He can still do the impossible. What we question is His willingness. Fear feeds on that uncertainty. It twists our pain into suspicion. It tries to convince us that the Lord who sees every sparrow fall[4] might overlook us.

But Jesus was not ignoring them. He was teaching them to look beyond the storm.

Some of the hardest seasons in life tempt us to pray the same words. "Don't You care?" Yet, it is often in those quiet stretches that His compassion becomes most real.

I have a dear friend who, in the span of seven months, lost three members of his immediate family. He's a fellow minister —a compassionate man who has comforted countless people through seasons of loss. But compiling three deaths in twelve months would stagger anyone.

The "Why, God?" question came naturally, not just for my friend, but for all of us who know and love him. We were all asking it. Why him? Why now? Why all three?

And the reality is, we don't have answers to those questions. There's no satisfying explanation for that kind of grief. No theological formula can make sense of losing your entire immediate family in a single year.

There's an old hymn that explains our anchor during seasons like that. Five verses, each beginning with a statement of what we don't know:

"I don't know why..."
"I don't know how..."
"I don't know what..."
"I don't know when..." [5]

And after each acknowledgment of our limitations, the songwriter quotes the Apostle Paul: "But I know whom I have believed, and am persuaded that he is able to keep that which I have committed unto him against that day."[6]

My friend couldn't explain why God allowed such devastation. However, he knew "Whom he had believed". And somehow, that was enough to keep him standing.

The timing of God is one of Scripture's great mysteries. In one of my Bibles, there is a blank page between Malachi and Matthew that has always intrigued me. That empty page represents four centuries. Scholars call them the Silent Years because no prophetic word came during that time. It appeared to the people of Israel that God had gone silent and was no longer working on their behalf.

I have never lived through four hundred years of silence, but I have endured weeks or months in which a single word from the Lord would have strengthened me. Instead, I felt dry and alone.

History tells us that during those 400 years, God was far from idle. In those years, He raised Alexander the Great to create a common language that would allow the Gospel to be shared with people from every nation. Then He ordained Rome to build roads that would one day carry the Gospel across the world.

And then, 400 years later, "*When the right time came, God sent his Son, born of a woman.*"[7] He speaks at the right time.

Our faith needs to hold on to that truth. His silence is never abandonment. His delay is never detachment. Often, the quiet season becomes the place where faith is tested before testimony arrives.

The disciples would soon hear His voice rise above the storm. When they did, they would understand that His stillness had never meant He was absent.

————

FAITH IN THE WRONG DIRECTION

When Jesus asked, "Do you still have no faith?"[8] He was not suggesting they had no faith. Their faith was very active, but it was placed on the wrong thing. They trusted the storm to swamp them. They trusted the waves to sink them. They trusted the darkness pressing in on them. Their belief was working, just not in the direction of the One who had spoken.

Fear isn't the absence of faith. It is faith pointed toward the wrong thing. Fear convinces us that danger carries more authority than our Savior. It tells us the storm is stronger than the One who spoke the promise of crossing over the Sea of Galilee.

Fear isn't the absence of faith. It is faith pointed toward the wrong thing.

The disciples did what we all tend to do. They trusted what they could see, hear, and feel. The wind howled. The boat shuddered. Their heads filled with the picture of their own ending. Because the storm felt real, fear felt like a proper response. Panic came through their experience, and it took up residence in their thoughts.

Yet Jesus had spoken over them before the first wave ever rose. *"Let us go to the other side."* That was the promise. That was the direction. That was the anchor they lost sight of once the sky turned black.

This is the trap we fall into so easily. We treat the storm as if it holds the final vote. We listen to the wind as if it has more say than the One who created it. Our attention drifts from His voice to our interpretation of the moment. And wherever our attention goes, our faith follows.

It is so easy for us to do. We "believe" the doctor's report more than the God who heals. We "believe" the numbers on the bank statement more than the One who provides. We "believe" the brokenness we feel more than the Redeemer who restores. Our faith is still present, but it is misplaced.

Jesus did not question them to shame them. He was revealing the real struggle they were having. The surrounding storm could not sink that boat, but the storm inside them could. The danger was not in the water. It was in the way they interpreted the water.

Faith that faces the wrong direction leads to paralysis and confusion. Faith that leans toward Him brings clarity and peace. The waves were loud, but their mistrust was louder. He addressed their fear before He addressed the storm.

While they trembled, He slept. His stillness startled them. Their panic soared. Their fear accused Him of not caring. However, His quiet posture communicated something else entirely. He trusted His Father. He knew the storm had limits.

His sleep was instruction. It showed a different way to live, not untouched by storms, but unharmed by them. Not unaware of danger, but unmoved by it. He was forming the same kind of peace within them. A peace that grows from knowing Who holds the boat and Who sets the destination.

They would learn it slowly. So do we. His rest that night was not merely an example. It was an invitation. He not only calms storms. He teaches His followers how to have peace in them.

The lesson was already taking shape before the sea grew quiet. The peace He displayed was the peace He meant to give them. And us.

———

BEFORE THE NEXT WAVE

Before the next storm rises, prepare your heart with truth that can steady you when fear begins to whisper its version of your story.

Take a few minutes to write down three anchors:

First, choose one scripture that reminds you of God's faithfulness. It might be a promise He's given, a truth about His character, or a declaration of His presence. Write it where you can see it regularly.

Second, record one specific way God has proven His care

for you in the past. Not a general statement, but a detailed memory of His provision, His timing, or His intervention. When fear suggests God has forgotten you, this memory becomes evidence that He has not.

Third, write one truth about God's character that the storm cannot change. He is sovereign. He is good. He is present. He is faithful. Fear will try to convince you otherwise, but this truth stands regardless of what the waves are doing.

When fear begins to rewrite your story, interrupt it with these truths. Speak them out loud. Repeat them until your breathing slows and your thoughts settle. Fear loses much of its power when truth has a voice louder than the storm.

You cannot stop fear from knocking at the door of your heart. But you can refuse to let it narrate your future.

———

REFLECT:

1. **"Fear magnifies the waves we were meant to walk through."** What "wave" in your life currently looks bigger than it actually is because fear has magnified it? What would change if you saw it from Jesus' perspective instead?

2. **The disciples asked, "Teacher, don't You care that we're perishing?"** When you're in crisis, what assumption about God's character do you struggle with most—His awareness, His care, or His ability to help? Why do you think that particular doubt surfaces for you?

3. **"Fear isn't the absence of faith. It's faith pointed toward the wrong thing."** What are you currently trusting more than God—a worst-case scenario, someone else's opinion, your own ability to fix things, or something else? How can you redirect that trust back to Jesus?

4. **The chapter mentions God's timing during the "Silent Years" between Malachi and Matthew.** Describe a season when God seemed silent in your life. Looking back, what was He doing behind the scenes that you couldn't see at the time?

5. **"Our faith needs to hold on to that truth. His silence is never abandonment."** If God feels silent or distant right now, what past evidence of His faithfulness can you remind yourself of while you wait?

PRACTICE:

Write down your three anchors (from the chapter's closing exercise). Post these somewhere you'll see them daily. When fear whispers its version of your story, speak these truths out loud.

- One Scripture that reminds you of God's faithfulness
- One specific memory of how God proved His care for you in the past
- One truth about God's character that the storm cannot change

CHAPTER 4

THE SLEEPING SAVIOR

God's peace is not the absence of storms but confidence in His sovereignty.

"But He was in the stern, asleep on a pillow." (Mark 4:38 KJV)

MOLLY LEE WAS A PASSENGER ON A FLIGHT FROM Charlotte to New York when she noticed a woman across the aisle who was terrified. The woman was crying, gripping her armrest with white knuckles, her breathing quick and shallow. Every sound the plane made seemed to send fresh waves of panic through her.

Flight attendant Floyd Dean-Shannon noticed too. He could have offered a quick word of encouragement and moved on. Instead, he sat down next to her.

For nearly ten minutes, he held her hand and spoke to her with quiet reassurance. Every time she heard a noise and asked, "What's that?" he'd calmly explain: "That's okay. That's just the jet bridge pulling away" or "That's just the landing gear retracting. We're fine."

With every question, he repeated the same message: "I got you. I'm going to be there for you. You're safe."

Molly Lee, watching from her seat, later said, "He didn't have to do that. To just see someone extend their heart in that way to a stranger was beautiful."

The woman's circumstances hadn't changed. The plane was still flying. The sounds were still happening. But she wasn't alone in her fear anymore. And somehow, that changed everything.[1]

That's the picture Mark gives us in the middle of the storm on Galilee. While the disciples panicked, convinced they were about to die, Jesus rested in the stern of the boat with a peace they couldn't understand.

That contrast carries us straight into the next part of the story, where their question becomes the same one we ask when life feels like it is taking on water.

Where is Jesus when the waves rise?

Every believer eventually arrives at that question. When the winds of life pull at everything familiar, and the water begins to fill the spaces we thought were secure, our hearts lean toward one concern. We know His promises. We quote them. He said He would be with us to the end of the age. He told us He would never leave us. Yet we still encounter days when His presence seems hidden, and His silence feels heavy.

We know His promises. We quote them. He said He would be with us to the end of the age. He told us He would never leave us. Yet we still encounter days when His presence seems hidden, and His silence feels heavy.

So where was He that night? The answer is simple. He was in the boat. Not pacing. Not shouting. Not scrambling for help. He lay in the stern with His head on a cushion, resting as if the lake were smooth and the night still.

To the disciples, that must have felt impossible. They were convinced they were about to die, yet He slept through the chaos that terrified them. His sleep, however, was not a signal of His indifference. It was the quiet confidence of someone who trusted His Father completely.

His rest was certainly practical. He had poured Himself out in teaching and healing. We will discover it was also intentional. Absolutely intentional. His rest would become the lesson they would remember long after the storm was gone.

His sleep revealed the difference between human fear and Divine assurance. It showed what life looks like when we trust Him more than we focus on our troubles. It offered a picture of peace that does not change when the sky grows dark.

This chapter turns our attention to that picture. In Chapter 3, we focused on the disciples' fear. In this chapter, we will discover a lesson for anyone who has ever wondered whether God sees the storm that surrounds them.

———

RESISTANCE FROM THE STORM

Unfortunately, hardship does not soften simply because we walk with Jesus. That night on the lake made that painfully clear. The storm didn't quiet itself because He stepped into the boat. The waves didn't shrink back out of reverence. The wind didn't change its tone in honor of the One who created it. The storm kept coming. It rose around Him with the same force that terrified the disciples.

Yet Jesus slept.

Water splashed over the sides and pooled at His feet. The hull trembled under the strain. The boat lifted and dropped as if the lake wanted to break it apart. Still, He rested in the stern, His head on a small cushion, untouched by the uproar that had stolen the disciples' breath.

That scene reveals something profound. Jesus wasn't pretending the storm didn't exist. His calmness flowed from a confidence that ran deeper than the waves. The disciples looked at the danger. He looked to His Father. What shook them could not unsettle Him because His trust held firm.

This is the rest He invites us to discover. A rest that grows from surrender. A rest that doesn't depend on silence in the sky, but on stillness in our hearts. Jesus spoke of it when He said, *"Come to Me... and I will give you rest."*[2]

The word He used, *anapauó*, carries the idea of relief. It is a picture of a tired traveler pausing long enough to catch his breath. In today's language, it sounds like someone saying, "Take a moment," "Catch your breath," or "Lay down what is wearing you out." It is rest that restores rather than simply pauses life.[3]

In 1929, Coca-Cola introduced a phrase in an advertising campaign that captures the meaning of *anapauó*. The ad reminded people that Coke was "the pause that refreshes." In the middle of the Great Depression, people needed a moment to step away from the heaviness of their lives, a simple break that would help them gather themselves for what came next. The campaign encouraged them that drinking a Coca-Cola could give them that pause.[4]

The Apostle Paul uses the same word, *anapauō*, to describe the comfort Philemon brought to weary believers. *"Your love has given me much joy and comfort... your kindness has often refreshed the hearts of God's people."*[5] His presence gave people a place to breathe again.

However, Jesus takes the picture even further. After inviting us to rest, He extends a second invitation: *"Take My yoke upon you."* The word "take" is *airō*, which describes an intentional act, the kind where you choose to shoulder something for a purpose.[6]

The yoke was a simple wooden bar that joined two animals so the work could be shared. One ox didn't carry the entire strain. Their strength was bound together.[7]

That is the picture Jesus gives. When we join ourselves to Him, the weight we carry doesn't disappear, but it shifts. His strength steadies our weakness and our worry. Rest grows not because the load is gone, but because we no longer pull alone.

Jesus could sleep in the storm because His life was joined with His Father. Their unity held Him steady. The storm never threatened what that bond had joined. That same partnership is what He offers to us. It is rest that stands firm while the wind rises. It is confidence that grows in the company of the One who holds authority over all things.

Storms never intimidate Jesus. They reveal Him and the rest He brings to weary souls, the kind that settles into us even while the waves continue to rise.

THE POSTURE OF TRUST

That posture of rest reveals what trust actually looks like.

Trust carries a certain posture. It does not rush or tremble. It does not flail in all directions. It looks a lot like Jesus resting in the stern. Quiet. Steady. Centered.

The disciples saw water climbing the sides of the boat. Jesus saw His Father's hand above the waves. Their situation was the same, yet their postures could not have been more different. Fear pulled the disciples into frantic movement. Trust allowed Jesus to settle into stillness because He was confident that His Father would handle what they could not.

That is the heart of trust. It holds to what God has spoken, even when conditions challenge every word. Trust does not pretend the storm is harmless. It simply refuses to let the storm decide the ending.

Trust does not pretend the storm is harmless. It simply refuses to let the storm decide the ending.

Jesus had already said they were going to the other side. Trust rested on that. Fear heard the same promise and collapsed. Both faced the same wind and spray. Only one carried peace.

Trust kept Jesus aligned with His Father. What rattled the disciples did not unsettle Him. He was not detached. He was anchored in the security of the Father's promise. The Scriptures use the image of an anchor only once, where we are told, *"We have this hope as an anchor for the soul, firm and secure."*[8]

The picture behind that verse is practical and beautiful. Sailors once used a small anchor called a kedge when a ship was stuck, and the wind refused to help. A rowboat carried the anchor ahead into deeper water and set it firmly in the seabed. Then the crew pulled the vessel forward hand over hand. Progress did not depend on the breeze. It came from the strength of what held them.[9]

Kedging offers a picture of hope in hard seasons. When life refuses to move, and circumstances will not cooperate, you can still draw your soul forward by holding to what God has spoken. You pull toward the promise, not because the situation eases, but because the anchor holds.

After describing our *"hope as an anchor for the soul"*, the writer of Hebrews continues, *"It enters the inner sanctuary behind the curtain, where our forerunner, Jesus, has entered on our behalf."*[10] He has gone ahead. He sits at the Father's right hand, guiding us into the presence where healing grows and burdens lift. Faith becomes steady when it is tied to Him, the way ancient ships steadied themselves in deep water.

The old hymn says it well:

> *I've anchored in Jesus; the storms of life I'll brave.*
> *I've anchored in Jesus; I fear no wind or wave.*
> *I've anchored in Jesus, for He has power to save.*
> *I've anchored in the Rock of Ages.*[11]

Jesus' heart was joined to His Father the way an anchor grips the foundations of the sea. That connection made Him unshakeable. Trust often looks simple on the outside. It may show up as quiet. It may show up as stillness. It can even show up as sleep.

Many believers misunderstand rest. It is not giving up. It

is giving over. When you rest in God, you deliberately place yourself under His strength and care. You let His peace take the lead instead of your own striving.

Trust speaks to the soul with a steady voice: *The storm is real, yet God is greater.* The waves rise high, yet His word rises higher. The pressure weighs heavily, yet I am not carrying it alone.

The disciples were exhausted because they were trying to pull the load themselves. Fear kept its grip on the helm, and fatigue followed closely behind. Trust releases that grip. It steadies the heart.

When Jesus finally stood and spoke to the storm, He rose from a place of peace rather than panic. His authority flowed from rest. That is the posture He teaches. Rest before rescue. Trust before triumph. Calm before command.

That is the posture He teaches. Rest before rescue. Trust before triumph. Calm before command.

Trust is not what we feel when the sky clears. Trust is what we choose while the storm is still rising. It anchors and steadies us. Trust loosens fear's hold and fastens our hope to the One who holds us fast.

———

THE THEOLOGY OF THE PILLOW

Mark includes a detail that many readers skim past: *"He was in the stern, asleep on a pillow."*[12] It sounds ordinary, almost too ordinary for a miracle story. Yet it is loaded with meaning. Jesus slept on a *proskephalaion*, a small leather cushion sailors kept on board to soften the hard planks beneath them.[13] It was the kind of object you would find on almost any ship. Nothing luxurious. Nothing impressive. Just a simple cushion used by working men.

That is the beauty of it. His peace did not depend on ideal surroundings. He was not stretched out on a comfortable mattress or tucked into a quiet room. He rested on a sailor's pillow while a storm roared around Him. His pillow became a sermon. It showed that peace is not found in a perfect environment. Peace is found in a Person. And wherever that Person is, rest becomes possible.

Jesus slept with a deep confidence that did not rise or fall with the circumstances surrounding Him. The pillow became a quiet pulpit, offering a message the disciples would remember long after the sea grew calm: "You do not need better conditions. You need a stronger confidence. Peace is not the end of the storm. Peace is the fruit of staying close to the One who rules over it."

The pillow also teaches us something else. Rest is not merely a break from the journey. It is part of it. Jesus moved at the Father's pace. He worked when the Father worked. He paused when the Father paused. He refused to let chaos set His schedule. The storm did not provoke Him into hurried action. It did not drive Him out of the Father's rhythm. The disciples reacted to every wave. Jesus remained aligned with His Father.

We often do the opposite. Trouble hits, and we rush to fix it. We scramble to control what feels out of control. The theology of the pillow invites us to pause instead of panic. It teaches us to breathe before we react. The disciples responded out of fear. Jesus responded out of fellowship. They fought against the storm. He rested in the Father's presence.

The theology of the pillow invites us to pause instead of panic. It teaches us to breathe before we react.

There is also a lesson in spiritual maturity here. Growth shows itself not only in what we do, but in how we rest. Jesus embraced the spaces God gave Him, even in a boat that pitched back and forth. His rest was not indifference. It was trust. He understood that quietness can be part of God's work, even when storms rage.

When we learn this, we begin to move with Jesus instead of rushing ahead of Him. We learn to rest beside Him instead of collapsing apart from Him. We discover that God's work is steady, confident, and never frantic. His peace is not fragile. It is not threatened by waves or wind.

———

BUT WHAT ABOUT DOUBT?

Before leaving this chapter, we should talk about the part of trust we rarely mention. We have explored rest, peace, and the quiet confidence Jesus modeled on the boat. But many believers wrestle with something that feels far less noble. They struggle with doubt.

Craig Groeschel captures this well: "The strongest faith

isn't a faith that never doubts. Rather, it's a faith that grows through doubts."[14]

Scriptures confirm that doubt shows up often in the lives of people God uses. Abraham laughed at God's promise. In the Exodus, Israel questioned Him after nearly every miracle. John the Baptist sent messengers to ask if Jesus was truly the One. And Thomas could not believe without evidence.

Matthew tells us that when Jesus appeared after the resurrection, *"they worshiped Him, but some doubted."*[15] Don't miss that the "they" in this verse is the eleven remaining disciples. This was not a large group of people, but rather the inner circle. Think about that. They saw the risen Christ with their own eyes, yet some hearts still wrestled with uncertainty. And, interestingly, Jesus did not scold them or withdraw His call because of their doubt. Instead, He entrusted the Great Commission to all of them, worshipers and doubters alike.

Doubt does not disqualify you from God's story. It often deepens your desire for clarity. The patron Saint of Doubt, Thomas, is a perfect example. He missed the first resurrection appearance, and when told about it, he could not bring himself to believe the others. *"'We have seen the Lord!' But he replied, 'I won't believe it unless I see the nail wounds in his hands, put my fingers into them, and place my hand into the wound in his side.'"*[16] We don't know what caused Thomas to have so much doubt, but it is apparent that His heart had been bruised by disappointment.

When Jesus appeared again eight days later, I find it interesting that Thomas did not have a chance to repeat his previous demands. He did not have to. Even though He wasn't present when Thomas expressed his doubt, Jesus must have heard every word. He invited Thomas to touch His wounds and see the truth for himself. Jesus had heard him long before He answered him.

That is the gift of honest doubt. It can draw us toward an encounter rather than away from it. Pretending keeps us at a distant. Honesty brings us close. We doubt because life hands us situations we cannot explain, but doubt does not have to harden our hearts. Our doubts can open our hearts if we bring them to Him.

The writer of Hebrews reminds us that faith carries us through hardship, confusion, and long seasons without answers. He urges us to fix our eyes on Jesus, the Author and Finisher of our faith.[17] Faith is not certainty. Faith is movement. It is walking toward Jesus even when your steps feel unsteady.

Doubt is a valley, not a destination. *"Yea, though I walk through the valley of the shadow...."*[18] We move **through** the valley, we do not remain in it. If you are wrestling with questions, it does not necessarily mean your faith is falling apart. It may mean your faith is growing roots. You are reaching for something real. You are seeking the One who hears even what you never say aloud.

And in that search, you might discover what Thomas discovered. The place where faith trembles can become the place where faith is transformed. The Savior who sleeps during storms is also the Savior who meets doubters with open arms.

———

Their trust had been stretched thin in the storm, and doubt had risen right alongside it. Yet neither trust nor doubt ended their story. These men had watched Jesus sleep and struggled to make sense of His calm. They learned, little by little, what it meant to rest near Him instead of reacting against the storm around them. They also discovered that honest doubt can lead a disciple closer to the Lord when it is carried to His feet. The pillow had whispered peace. The yoke had taught them how to lean.

Another lesson waited just ahead. It was one they never could have predicted, because the same Jesus who rested in the stern was about to rise with authority that belonged to no one else.

His rest revealed confidence. His voice would soon reveal Kingship.

Up to this point, the disciples had only seen Him respond to what was broken. He healed the sick. He taught the crowds. He confronted darkness. But what happened next would leave them shaken in a new way. Jesus did not merely work within creation. He commanded it.

The storm had pushed against their boat, yet His word would push against their understanding of Who shared the boat with them. This chapter has shown us the Savior who rests. The next will show us the Savior who rules. The One who lay quietly on a sailor's cushion is the same One who can speak to the wind itself.

The disciples, soaked and shaking, were moments away from a revelation that would change how they thought about fear, faith, and the authority of Christ.

Step into the next chapter. The storm has not eased. But Jesus is about to rise.

———

REFLECT:

1. **Jesus slept through the storm while the disciples panicked.** What do you think the difference was between them? What would it look like for you to rest in God's presence even while your circumstances rage?

2. **The chapter explores the Greek word *anapauō* (rest/refresh).** When was the last time you experienced true rest—not just physical sleep, but soul-level refreshment in God's presence? What prevents you from regularly accessing that kind of rest?

3. **"Trust carries a certain posture. It doesn't rush or tremble."** Honestly assess your current posture before God. Are you frantic, striving, anxious? Or are you resting, waiting, trusting? What would need to shift for you to move toward a posture of trust?

4. **The yoke metaphor teaches us that Jesus shares the load.** What burden are you trying to carry alone that Jesus is inviting you to share with Him? What makes it hard for you to let Him carry part of the weight?

5. **"The theology of the pillow" shows that peace doesn't depend on ideal surroundings.** Where are you waiting for circumstances to change before you'll allow yourself to have peace? What if peace isn't found in better conditions but in deeper connection with Jesus?

6. **The chapter addresses honest doubt.** What question or doubt have you been afraid to bring to God? Thomas received an encounter when he

brought his doubts to Jesus. What might happen if you voiced yours honestly?

PRACTICE:

- **Kedging exercise:** When you feel stuck and the wind refuses to help, identify one promise of God that's already set firm ahead of you. For the next week, "pull yourself forward" by meditating on that promise, even when circumstances don't cooperate. Write down what shifts in your heart as you do this.

CHAPTER 5

THE VOICE THAT
STILLED THE WIND

**_His rest revealed His confidence. His voice
revealed His kingship._**

*"When Jesus woke up, he rebuked the wind and said to the waves,
'Silence! Be still!' Suddenly the wind stopped, and there was a great
calm." (Mark 4:39)*

———

THE STORM HAD NOT EASED. THE WIND STILL PUSHED
against the boat, and the waves kept rising with a force that
pounded fear into every man on board. Darkness pressed
around them with a heaviness that felt almost alive. The disciples stood soaked and shaking, their hands sore from fighting
a battle they could not win. Their shouts had faded. Their
strength was spent.

Then Jesus stood.

A moment earlier, He had been resting in the stern. Now,

He rose with a calm that did not belong to the night around them. They had watched Him teach crowds and heal broken bodies. They had watched demons flee at His command. Yet nothing had prepared them for this quiet moment when He rose to His feet and faced the storm.

Jesus did not lift His voice in fear. He did not match the storm's volume. The One who shaped the sky with a word did not need to wrestle with the force behind the elements. He needed only to speak to them.

And the storm heard Him. The same voice that had called creation into being and summoned the dead back to life now spoke to the wind and sea. What the disciples could not overcome through their efforts or experiences, Jesus calmed with a single command. His words cut through the night with the clarity of a sudden light.

But this was unlike anything they had witnessed. People had resisted Him. Demons had protested. But creation responded without argument.

When the water grew quiet, it happened with a speed that stole their breath. The calm was not gradual. It was immediate. And there was no mistaking that it was of Divine origin.

Yet the greater storm inside them was calmed. They were filled with awe as they realized that the peace they were seeking was not in the sea. It was found in the Savior who ruled it. And we can discover that as well.

In this chapter, we will stand beside those weary and wet disciples. We will explore the moment that changed everything. Because the One who silenced the waters that night still speaks to the storms in our lives. His authority has not weakened. His word still overturns chaos.

———

JESUS AROSE AND REBUKED

Despite the disciples' experience at sea and their efforts to survive, the wind did not soften, nor did the darkness retreat. It was as if an invisible hand gripped the night and refused to let go.

Then Jesus stood.

The moment He rose to His feet, something shifted, not in the storm at first, but in them. Just His presence brought calm to the situation. The wind still howled, but it was no longer the loudest thing in the boat. The waves still attacked, but their fury felt strangely diminished. The storm had not changed, but the atmosphere had. The disciples were no longer looking at the waves. They were looking at the One who controlled them.

Jesus positioned Himself with the quiet certainty of Someone who knows the battle has already been decided. His rising was in itself an act of authority. He refused to be intimidated by forces that terrified everyone else.

Then He spoke. But not to the storm as they understood it.

Mark says Jesus "rebuked" the wind. The word is *epitimaō*, and in Scripture it is consistently the language of confrontation: sharp, decisive, and authoritative.[1] It is the word Jesus used to silence demons, command unclean spirits, or confront evil directly. As Rick Renner notes, *epitimaō* "means to speak dishonorably to someone; to sternly speak against; to chide; to rebuke.... He didn't stand up and say, 'I rebuke you, wind!' On the contrary, He stood up and began to verbally assassinate the wind. That is, He had a conversation with the unseen spiritual force behind the storm, and with His words He assaulted, belittled, demeaned, and humiliated it."[2]

Those who played competitive sports understand this

kind of confrontation. In basketball, we called it trash-talk, speaking with such confidence and intimidation that your opponent's focus shifts from playing their best to simply trying to prove you wrong. However, Jesus wasn't engaging in psychological games. He was exercising sovereign authority over spiritual forces, confronting them with the kind of direct, intimidating speech that left no room for resistance.

He didn't rebuke the weather. He rebuked the source behind it.

The disciples were fighting water. Jesus was confronting wickedness. They were battling on the surface. Jesus was addressing the root. What terrified them physically, He confronted spiritually. And here is the power of that moment: when Jesus speaks to the source, the symptoms have no choice but to obey.

The disciples were fighting water. Jesus was confronting wickedness.

There is something breathtaking about this moment. The men in the boat had exhausted themselves fighting what they could see. Jesus rose and dealt with what they couldn't see. They were bailing water. He was binding the adversary behind the waves.

This is where discipleship becomes real: Your efforts may manage symptoms, but only His authority breaks the source.

When Jesus arose and rebuked, the storm had already lost. His voice carried the weight of heaven and the force of sovereignty. No unseen enemy could stand beneath the authority of the One who commanded the unseen as effortlessly as He commands the sea.

For the rest of their lives, the disciples would recall this night: a night when the wind bowed, the waves obeyed, and the tempest fell silent. All because Jesus arose and rebuked the source of the storm.

———

THE LANGUAGE OF COMMAND

When Jesus finally spoke, His words did not rise from panic or exhaustion. They came from a position of authority.

"Silence! Be still!"[3]

The Sea of Galilee, moments from swallowing the boat whole, collapsed into stillness.

The language He used is striking. In Greek, Jesus' command is *phimōthēti*, "to muzzle."[4] It is the same word used when Jesus shut down demons who attempted to speak out of turn.[5] It is not gentle language. It is not soothing language. It is restraining language, fierce, authoritative, and decisive.

Rick Renner writes, "...this phrase is difficult to translate... in effect means to muzzle; to silence; or to still. Actually, the very best way to explain it is to say that Jesus muzzled the sea, telling it to 'shhh'."[6]

Jesus wasn't shushing the wind like a librarian quieting a noisy room. Like a master stopping a ferocious animal, he was silencing the adversary. What the disciples saw as weather, Jesus treated as something that required spiritual restraint. This is the language of a King.

When He spoke, He addressed the chaos the same way a commander confronts an uprising: with the expectation of immediate obedience. No negotiation. No explanation. Simply a command backed by the full weight of heaven.

And creation bowed.

Authority without volume still works today.

On January 15, 2009, US Airways Flight 1549 struck a flock of geese moments after takeoff from LaGuardia Airport near New York City. Both engines failed. The Airbus A320 was carrying 155 passengers and crew, and it was going down over one of the most densely populated cities on earth.

In the cockpit, alarms were blaring. Warning lights flashed across the instrument panel. The plane was losing altitude fast, and there was no time to reach any airport. Captain Chesley "Sully" Sullenberger had seconds to make a decision that would determine whether everyone on board lived or died.

The cockpit voice recorder captured what happened next. In the midst of chaos, Sullenberger's voice came through with an almost eerie calm. No screaming. No panic. Just a flat, authoritative monotone stating the decision he'd already made: "We're gonna be in the Hudson."

His first officer, Jeffrey Skiles, didn't question it. The flight attendants didn't hesitate. The crew executed the emergency water landing with precision, following Sullenberger's commands exactly as he gave them. One hundred fifty-five people walked away from what should have been a catastrophic crash.[7]

Sullenberger knew that authority in a crisis doesn't come from volume. It comes from certainty. His crew didn't need him to yell. They needed him to know what to do and to say it with the kind of clarity that left no room for doubt.

And this is where we begin to understand the language of

command: Jesus does not yell to compete with noise. He commands because the universe recognizes His voice.

Volume doesn't equal authority. Authority is in who's speaking and the certainty behind their words.

That's the language Jesus used on the Sea of Galilee. He didn't raise His voice to compete with the storm. He spoke with the calm assurance of Someone who knew the wind would obey.

Behind the English words "Peace, be still" lies the force of sovereign speech. Peace isn't merely the outcome. It is the authority behind the order. When Jesus declared peace, He wasn't describing a condition. He was imposing a verdict. When He said, "Be still," He wasn't offering a suggestion. He was issuing a spiritual cease-and-desist order.

In that moment, the disciples witnessed what Psalm 33 had foretold: *"He spoke, and it came to be; He commanded, and it stood firm."*[8]

The One in their boat used the same creative voice that called galaxies into orbit. He spoke with the same commanding presence that summoned Lazarus from the grave. The same dominion that shut the mouths of demons now muzzled a storm determined to take them under.

The One in their boat used the same creative voice that called galaxies into orbit. He spoke with the same commanding presence that summoned Lazarus from the grave.

His word is not instruction. It is an intervention. His authority is not symbolic. It is supreme. The disciples had pleaded for survival. Jesus spoke from a position of sovereignty. They had bailed water. He rewrote the weather.

In a world full of noise, storms, voices, and threats, this truth remains unshaken: Nothing in creation ignores the voice of its Creator. And that should bring us comfort in our storms.

He still speaks with the same commanding voice today. He shushes the roar of a doctor's prognosis that stirs the winds of fear. He quiets the sudden waves of financial strain when expenses crash without warning. He settles the noisy ache of broken relationships and the confusion that follows separation.

Wherever the storm rages, His authority remains unchanged. And if you listen closely in the midst of your struggle, you'll hear the calm, steady whisper of the Savior who still says, "Shhhhh."

———

REBUKING THE SOURCE, NOT THE SYMPTOM

This language of command reveals something crucial about the storm itself. In Chapter 2, we looked closely at the word Mark used to describe how the storm "beat against" the boat, *epiballō*. Let me remind you that the verb wasn't typical language for wind-driven waves. It wasn't meteorological. It was personal and confrontational. In classical Greek, the word carried the idea of an entity striking, an aggressor attacking, or an adversary throwing force against another.

That detail matters. The storm wasn't just water moving unpredictably. It wasn't merely a clash of pressure systems over Galilee. Scripture points to something deeper, unseen hostility pushing against the command of Jesus and the people He called to cross the sea.

This is why Jesus didn't speak to the storm like a sailor pleading with the weather. He rebuked it. He treated the wind and waves as if Someone stood behind them. And He was right.

We often forget that following Jesus does not place us in a spiritually neutral world. As followers of Jesus, we are drawn into a larger conflict in which unseen forces seek to hinder God's purpose and derail God's people. Paul warned us that *"we are not fighting against flesh-and-blood enemies, but against evil rulers and authorities of the unseen world, against mighty powers in this dark world, and against evil spirits in the heavenly places."*[9] Difficulties in life may appear circumstantial, but often there is a spiritual undercurrent attempting to intimidate us, distract us, or exhaust our faith.

Jesus understood that. He refused to waste His energy battling symptoms. He confronted the adversary behind the waves.

This matters because storms in our lives often come with voices. These voices are not always audible; they are most often internal. That voice sounds like fear. Or accusation. Or despair. The voice that taunts us, "You won't make it to the other side."

Bonnie Martin is a licensed counselor who helps victims of violence and trafficking find healing. Years ago, during a painful collapse in her marriage, she went on a mission trip to South Africa with her father just to come up for air. On their last day, they visited a wildlife reserve and found themselves standing just two feet from a lion, separated only by a chain-link fence. Trying to lighten the moment, Bonnie said, "Hey, kitty, kitty."

She didn't expect what came next.

The lion lunged. Its roar hit the fence with such force that she said her "nerves caught fire." Later, she learned a lion's roar is meant to intimidate, to assert dominance, to claim territory.

That's when the Holy Spirit whispered to her heart: "Bonnie, Satan walks around like a roaring lion. But do you see that fence? That fence is the blood of Jesus. He may roar, but he cannot touch you. He is the one in the cage. You are the one who is free. But you've been living as if it were the other way around."[10]

The roar of her pain was loud, but it was not the source of her struggle. Just like the storm on Galilee.

Reacting to symptoms never wins spiritual battles. They are won by standing in the authority of Jesus and addressing the root. You can fix budgets, adjust schedules, negotiate relationships, and reorganize your life, but none of those things silence the spiritual pressure behind the storm. Only Jesus does that. Only His word cuts through the invisible as it confronts the visible.

His rebuke reached farther than the disciples ever realized. He was not merely calming a lake; He was disrupting hell's strategy. He was not simply stopping a storm; He was silencing the adversary.

And the sea obeyed.

———

A PRACTICAL WORD FOR OUR STORMS

Many of us spend our emotional and spiritual energy battling the surface struggles—the doctor's report, the financial strain, the fractured relationship, the anxious thoughts that tighten in our chests. But the real battle is often deeper. That is why it is crucial that we discern the source and don't simply manage the symptoms.

When fear surges, pray, "Jesus, silence every voice but Yours." When anxiety circles, declare His authority: "Lord, muzzle the storm behind this storm." When discouragement rises, anchor in His word rather than your worry.

Jesus didn't teach the disciples to manage the sea. He taught them to discern the battle. And He showed them that storms are never stronger than the Savior who confronts them.

When Jesus speaks to the source, the symptoms lose their power. And take heart! When He rises during your storm, it signifies that the storm has already begun to lose its grip.

————

WHEN HEAVEN'S VOICE CONFRONTS HELL'S NOISE

The storm had roared that night. Its voice screamed across the water with the fury of something that wanted to be heard. Fear has a way of drowning out reason. Every gust and every crash of water carried the same message: You're not going to make it.

Our fears still speak that way. Not with words you hear with your ears. Fear's voice comes as pressure, panic, and confusion. It stirs up a noise inside the soul that makes you question everything God has spoken.

> **Fear's voice comes as pressure, panic, and confusion. It stirs up a noise inside the soul that makes you question everything God has spoken.**

Then Jesus spoke, and His voice didn't compete with the storm; it confronted it. His authority collided with the intimidation of fear, and the difference was immediate. The wind didn't taper off. It didn't fade gradually. It ceased. The waves didn't settle slowly. They flattened. When Jesus' voice enters a storm, the noise that once seemed so powerful suddenly sounds small.

The disciples had cried above the storm. Jesus spoke into it. They reacted to the noise. Jesus released authority. They were victims of the chaos. He was sovereign over it.

And this is the part we often miss. While fear is meant to intimidate you, His peace is meant to define you.

The enemy uses noise—fear, accusations, lies, and worst-case scenarios—to flood the heart with uncertainty. Jesus uses His voice to restore clarity and peace. The storm roars to overwhelm you. Jesus speaks to reorient you and to remind you He still rules the wind.

And here's the truth hidden in this story: Peace is not the absence of noise. Peace is the supremacy of His voice. The disciples stood on the soaked deck, water dripping from their hair, breath catching in their throats. Only moments earlier, they were convinced they were going to die. Now the sea looked like polished glass. All of it changed because a single voice dared to confront what terrified them.

Jesus didn't avoid the noise. He answered it.

Most of us have a "storm soundtrack" playing in the background of our minds. It can be the quiet hum of worry or the whisper of regret. For many, it is the steady pulse of fear or insecurity. And most of us try to silence that noise by turning up the volume of our own efforts. We work harder to fix the problem. We push through with greater intensity. But the noise of the storm doesn't bow to our efforts. It will only bow to His authority.

So what do we do? Here is a simple tool I have found helpful. When anxiety rises, or circumstances scream to stir fear in our hearts, speak one sentence out loud that declares Jesus' authority over your internal storm.

Not a speech. Not a collection of verses. Just one sentence of truth.

"Jesus, speak peace over this fear."

"Lord, Your voice is stronger than this report."

"Calm my mind as You calmed the sea."

"Silence every voice but Yours."

Just one sentence spoken sincerely in faith taps into the resources of the Peace-Speaker.

This simple act shifts your heart's focus from the noise to the One who can silence it. It reminds you that Jesus, not your circumstances, has the final say.

The storm now lay still beneath the authority of Jesus' voice. The very thing that just moments earlier had appeared to be the catalyst of their destruction was now a source of revelation. They hadn't just survived the storm. They witnessed the sovereignty of the One who stood above it.

———

But the story doesn't end with the rebuke. There is a second miracle tucked quietly inside the first.

Mark tells us, *"There was a great calm."*[11] Not a partial calm. Not a gradual settling. But a mega calm. An unnatural, overwhelming stillness that carried the weight of heaven's touch. This wasn't the kind of peace that comes when a storm simply runs out of energy. This was the kind of peace only the Prince of Peace can produce.

And sometimes that is where the real work of God begins. Storms reveal our fear, but calm reveals our hearts. After the wind bowed and the waves obeyed, the disciples were left with a new kind of trembling. Awe. They asked the only question that made sense: "Who is this man?"

In the next chapter, we will move into the sacred quiet where Jesus does more than rescue. He reveals. The sea had been a source of fear. Now it became a mirror, and the disciples saw both His majesty and their own need more clearly than ever.

So, as you turn the page, the winds have stopped. But the wonder is just beginning.

———

REFLECT:

1. **Jesus rebuked the source (spiritual forces) rather than just the symptoms (wind and waves).** What "symptoms" are you currently battling (anxiety, conflict, financial pressure) when you should be addressing the spiritual source behind them? How might prayer change if you focused on the root instead of the fruit?

2. **The language Jesus used—*epitimaō* (rebuke) and *phimōthēti* (muzzle)—was fierce and**

authoritative. Does your prayer life reflect the authority Jesus has given you, or do you tend to beg, plead, or negotiate with circumstances? What would change if you prayed with greater confidence in His authority?

3. **"When Jesus speaks, everything—wind, waves, demons, death itself—has to obey."** What area of your life feels completely out of control right now? How does it change your perspective to remember that Jesus' voice has authority over even that?

4. **The chapter describes Hell's strategy: "to intimidate, distract, and exhaust your faith."** Which of these three tactics is the enemy using most effectively in your life right now? What would it look like to refuse that tactic?

5. **"Peace is not the absence of noise. Peace is the supremacy of His voice."** What "noise" is currently loudest in your mind—fear, accusation, worst-case scenarios, or something else? What is one sentence of truth you can speak out loud to let Jesus' voice become louder than the noise?

PRACTICE:

- One-sentence prayer tool: Identify your current internal storm (anxiety about finances, fear about health, uncertainty about relationships, etc.). Write one sentence that declares Jesus' authority over it. *Example: "Jesus, Your voice is louder than this diagnosis."* Speak it aloud every time fear rises this week. Track what happens to the noise in your mind.

CHAPTER 6

GREAT STORM — GREATER CALM

The storm revealed their fear.
The calm revealed His authority.

"When Jesus woke up, he rebuked the wind and said to the waves, 'Silence! Be still!' Suddenly the wind stopped, and there was a great calm." (Mark 4:39)

———

THE STORM DID NOT END THE WAY STORMS USUALLY DO.

It did not gradually cease blowing. There was no slow retreat of the wind. One moment, the Sea of Galilee was raging with violence. Next, it was completely still. This kind of stillness feels almost louder than the storm that preceded it. This stillness leaves you standing silent, searching for words to express how you feel, but you can't find them.

Mark tells us there was a great calm. This calm was not the natural settling that occurs when energy dissipates. This calm arrived fully formed, as sudden as the command that summoned it.

The disciples had just survived a great storm, but now they were facing something even more unsettling. The danger was gone, yet their hearts were racing faster than before. The waves no longer threatened them, but awe had taken its place. Fear had not disappeared. It had simply changed direction.

Storms terrify us because they reveal our vulnerability. But calm exposes something deeper. Calm compels us to confront the true nature of Jesus.

It's easy to cry out to God when the waves are crashing. Panic sharpens prayer. Desperation provides voice to faith. But what do you do when the wind stops? What happens when the crisis passes and silence settles in? That's often when the real questions surface. Not: *"Will we survive?"* But, *"Who is this?"*

The disciples were not prepared for the calm. They knew how to fight the storm, but not how to stand in the presence of a Savior whose authority reached beyond nature itself. The storm revealed their fear. The calm revealed His identity —and their own. Sometimes God's greatest work in us occurs not in the chaos we endure, but in the calm that follows.

———

FROM GREAT FEAR TO GREAT FAITH

The storm had threatened the disciples' lives. It also exposed their fears.

In verse 37, Mark described the storm as great, using the word *megas*. This wasn't a passing squall or a manageable challenge. It was overwhelmingly violent, beyond their ability to control. Even the seasoned fishermen were terrified by it. The waves were not merely rough. They were relentless.

It was a great wind that placed them in great danger. And they had great fear.

But the moment Jesus spoke, everything changed. The wind stopped. The waves slowed. Now Mark tells us there was a great calm. *"The wind ceased, and there was a great calm."*[1] The same word, *megas*, is used.

That detail matters because it reveals an essential aspect of how God works. The calm was not smaller than the storm. It was not a fragile relief that might give way again. The calm was equal in magnitude and greater in authority than the storm, because it did not come from nature running out of strength, but from Jesus exercising His Divine power.

That is the thing about the One who speaks to storms. For every *megas* storm, He provides a *megas* calm. For *megas* sickness, we have a *megas* Healer. For every *megas* emotional distress, we have a *megas* Peace-Speaker. For every *megas* relational fracture, we have a *megas* Restorer.

"There is no disease God cannot heal. There is no heart God cannot mend. There is no relationship God cannot restore. There is no person God cannot save. There is no pain God cannot redeem. There is no sin God cannot forgive. There is no bondage God cannot break. There is no need God cannot meet. There is no enemy God cannot defeat. There is no mountain God cannot move."[2]

This is where fear loses its grip. The disciples had been afraid because the storm exceeded their strength. Now they were standing in a calm that exceeded their understanding. They did not yet have all the answers. They did not yet fully grasp who Jesus was. Yet, something foundational had shifted.

Faith does not require the absence of fear; it requires a greater object than the source of our fear. The disciples moved from fear anchored in circumstances to faith anchored in Christ. The storm revealed the limits of their ability. The calm introduced them to the sufficiency of His sovereignty.

———

HEAVEN'S ARITHMETIC

We tend to measure life by human math. If the storm is great, we assume the damage will be greater. If the loss is severe, we brace for lasting pain. If the fear is overwhelming, we expect peace to be fragile at best.

That's how the world adds things up. However, heaven operates using a different set of principles.

One of the worst moments in my life began with a crashing sound around 9:00 in the morning.

Shirlene had taken our two oldest children to school, where she also taught part-time as a music instructor. I was home with our youngest son, Stephen, who was preschool age. He'd gone into the garage to get a toy when he spotted a fishing rod lying on top of a folded ping-pong table leaning against the wall.

Being all boy, he started climbing.

The table fell backward on top of him.

I rushed to the garage, saw my son lying underneath, and lifted the table off him. What happened next wasn't logical, but I was moving on pure instinct. I reached down, slid my hands under his arms, and lifted him.

His chest collapsed. As if he no longer had ribs. His eyes rolled back in his head.

All I could say was, *"Jesus, please help my baby! Please don't let him die!"*

I ran into the house, still holding Stephen, and called for

the visiting evangelist staying with us that week. "Maxie, I need you! Maxie!" He began to pray. I dialed 911, explained what happened, then made the call no parent wants to make: "Shirlene, come home immediately. There's been an accident with Stephen."

Sometime in all of that, between the prayer, the 911 call, and the panic, something happened.

Stephen moved in my arms. I noticed that he was moving and looked down at him. He looked normal.

The EMTs arrived before Shirlene and checked him over. "We can't find anything wrong with him," one said. The other walked out to the garage, saw the ping-pong table lying on the floor, and came back shaking his head. "That thing must weigh 200 pounds. It should have crushed the kid."

His partner nodded. "Well, there is absolutely nothing wrong with him."

Shirlene came rushing through the door, crying. Stephen jumped out of my arms, ran to her, and said, "I'm okay, Mom!"

I cannot show you X-rays of a crushed chest. I cannot produce scans of damaged internal organs. But I know what I felt when I picked him up. I felt his chest collapse under my hands. I saw his eyes roll back.

I experienced something that day that twelve men experienced two thousand years earlier. In my moment of terror, Jesus brought a great calm.

That's heaven's arithmetic. The crisis was overwhelming. The intervention was greater.

Throughout Scripture, God rarely responds in proportion to human standards. He responds abundantly. His provision is always greater than the need. His deliverance is unmistakable. When the darkness deepens, His light does not flicker. It shines brighter. When Israel stood trapped between Pharaoh's army and the Red Sea, God did not merely provide an escape. He opened the sea itself, turning overwhelming danger into unmistakable deliverance.[3] When Gideon's army was reduced to three hundred men against an overwhelming force, God did not simply balance the odds. He reversed them, proving that victory comes from His power, not human strength.[4]

God rarely responds in proportion to human standards. He responds abundantly. His provision is always greater than the need. His deliverance is unmistakable. When the darkness deepens, His light does not flicker. It shines brighter.

We see this pattern again and again. Great bondage met with greater deliverance. Great sin met with greater grace. Heaven's arithmetic never aims for balance. It aims for victory.

The disciples only hoped to survive. What they feared would destroy them became the very stage on which Jesus' authority was revealed.

And this matters deeply for us. When you find yourself in a storm that feels too heavy, too complex, and too relentless, it is tempting to assume that peace, if it comes at all, will arrive in small portions. A little relief here. A temporary break there. Just enough calm to get through the moment.

But Scripture invites us to believe for something greater. The calm Jesus brings carries more weight than the storm it replaces. God's power always exceeds what opposes it. What threatens you does not define your life. The authority of Jesus always supersedes every threat. And when He speaks, the outcome is never smaller than the problem.

———

LESSONS IN SPIRITUAL AUTHORITY

The storm obeyed Jesus instantly. The wind recognized His voice. The waves responded without hesitation. But the disciples were still trying to make sense of what had just happened. Authority had been displayed, but they had not yet fully understood it. Most of the time, spiritual authority, when first encountered, leaves us stunned before it leaves us confident.

Jesus didn't calm the storm to show off His power. He calmed it to teach His disciples who they were learning to trust. Authority, in the kingdom of God, is not something you wield to impress others. It is something you submit to before you ever exercise it.

Authority, in the kingdom of God, is not something you wield to impress others. It is something you submit to before you ever exercise it.

This is where many of us get confused. We talk about spiritual authority as if it were a position or certainty of tone. But Jesus did not have to remind nature that He was large and in charge. He spoke with the calm assurance of Someone who knew the Father was already backing every word.

True spiritual authority does not come from striving harder. Nor does it come from a position or title. It flows from alignment. When we live out of alignment with the Father, we forfeit any authority we may think we possess.

Jesus lived in constant union with the Father. He spoke when the Father spoke. He rested when the Father rested.[5] His authority over the storm was simply the overflow of a life lived in submission. Never forget that speaking with authority is always accompanied by living in submission. Jesus did not speak to dominate the sea. He spoke to obey the Father.

That changes how we understand authority in our own lives.

Spiritual authority is not granted to those who are loudest or the most gifted. It is entrusted to those who remain faithful in the quiet places. It is cultivated through prayer, shaped through obedience, and strengthened through trust. Authority grows in us long before it is ever expressed through us.

Spiritual authority is not granted to those who are loudest or the most gifted. It is entrusted to those who remain faithful in the quiet places.

The disciples had been given authority when Jesus called them, but they had not yet learned how to rest in it. They knew how to work. They knew how to row. They knew how to fight wind and water. But they had not yet learned how to stand still and trust the One who commanded it.

Perhaps that is the lesson for us as well.

Many of us exhaust ourselves fighting what Jesus intends to speak to. We try to manage storms that require His authority rather than our effort. We scramble for control when what is needed is alignment. The result is weariness and frustration—neither of which produces peace.

Jesus never invited His disciples to control the storm. He invited them to trust Him in it.

Spiritual authority begins there. Not with rebuking the wind, but with surrendering our hearts. Not with commanding circumstances, but with submitting to Christ. The deeper we trust His authority, the more confidently we can rest beneath it.

The storm taught the disciples that Jesus has authority over nature. The calm taught them that authority flows from relationship with the Father. And the question lingering in the silence was not, "How did He do that?" It was, "Who is He, and can we trust Him fully?"

That question still shapes every lesson in spiritual authority today.

————

WORSHIP THAT FOLLOWS THE WONDER

The storm was gone. The sea was still. And no one rushed to speak. Mark tells us the disciples eventually asked one another, *"Who is this man?"*[6] Their words expressed their wonder. I can imagine that, when all was calm, the disciples sat in silence for a few moments. The kind of silence that follows when something holy has just happened and you know better than to fill the space too quickly.

Worship often begins that way. We tend to think of worship as something we do, as songs we sing, words we speak, and actions we take. However, in Scripture, worship often starts as something that happens to us. It begins when we realize we have encountered more than we expected—

those moments when God reveals Himself in ways that will undo our categories and strengthen our hope.

The ancient story of Jonah reveals an often-forgotten truth: God can turn even our disobedience into an opportunity for His glory. When the sailors threw Jonah into the sea, it calmed. Then, something extraordinary happened! *"The sailors were awestruck by the Lord's great power, and they offered him a sacrifice and vowed to serve him."*[7] The Hebrew word for *awestruck* reveals a faith born from witnessing God's power.

Jonah's flight from God unexpectedly led these sailors to a life-changing encounter. Which then led to worship. It is an excellent reminder of how God's plans prevail, even through our failures. In our lives, mistakes and missteps can become Divine intersections where God shows Himself mightily. Even our imperfections can be woven into the greater tapestry of His redemptive work.

The disciples had followed Jesus for some time. They had heard Him teach. They had seen Him heal. They had watched demons flee at His command. This moment, however, was different. As we have seen, this was not compassion or power directed toward others. This was authority revealed up close and personally.

The wonder came first. The worship followed. They were no longer asking how to survive. They were asking who He truly was.

True worship is not driven by relief alone. Relief fades. Other difficulties arise in the future. Gratitude can drift as we eventually return to the routines of life. But wonder anchors the soul. When we see Jesus more clearly than before, worship becomes the only reasonable response. Not because we are commanded to worship, but because nothing else fits the moment.

The disciples were safe, but they were also changed. That is the kind of worship God desires. Not the hurried worship that moves quickly past mystery. Not the shallow worship that thanks God and moves on unchanged. Instead, it is the worship that lingers. Worship that listens. The kind of worship that starts with awe and culminates in submission.

When Jesus stills the storms in our lives, we are grateful. But when He reveals Himself through those storms, we are transformed. Worship becomes less about what He has done for us and more about who He has shown Himself to be.

That night on the Sea of Galilee, no altar was built. No song was recorded. No prayer was written down. Yet, worship happened all the same. It emerged as a hushed question, formed in the realization that God had been nearer than they ever understood.

When the storm has passed, there is often a pull to move forward too quickly, to explain what happened, or to get back to what feels normal. But some moments are meant to linger. Stay with the silence. Let it settle. Worship that grows out of wonder is not in a hurry to speak. It learns to rest in the nearness of God. And in that quiet place, faith takes on a deeper shape.

———

The storm had taken its toll. It unsettled what the disciples thought they knew and forced them to confront fears they didn't realize were there. However, the calm did something different. It stayed with them. It settled into the quiet that followed and lingered there, slowly changing how they understood Jesus and themselves.

They went into the storm hoping they would get through

it. They came out of it realizing they had come face-to-face with God.

That's often how it works for us. We ask God to stop the storm, convinced that peace will come with relief. But sometimes peace arrives another way. It comes when we recognize Who has been with us the entire time.

Even then, not everything was resolved. The questions that remained were no longer driven by fear but by meaning. Not *"Will we survive?"* but *"Who is this man?"*

The boat kept moving. The night hadn't yet given way to morning. The far shore was still ahead. Crossings rarely bring final answers. More often, they open the door to something deeper.

The disciples might have thought the storm was the challenge, the climax of the journey. They would discover that when the boat finally reached the far shore, the wind and waves were only part of the assignment. What awaited them next would test their faith in different ways. It would also help answer their question of "Who is this man?"

Jesus had brought them safely through the storm. Now, He would lead them into unfamiliar territory. The sea was calm. But the mission was just beginning.

———

REFLECT:

1. **"The storm revealed their fear; the calm revealed His authority."** What has a recent storm revealed about your faith? What did you discover about yourself—or about God—that you might not have seen any other way?

2. **Mark uses the word *megas* (great) for both the storm and the calm.** How does it encourage you to know that God's peace is equal in magnitude to whatever threatens you? Can you think of a time when God's intervention matched or exceeded the size of your problem?

3. **"Heaven's arithmetic" doesn't aim for balance but for victory.** Where have you been praying for God to simply "even things out" when He might be planning overwhelming provision or deliverance? What would it look like to pray with greater expectation?

4. **The chapter teaches that spiritual authority flows from relationship with the Father, not from position or volume.** How aligned is your life with the Father's will right now? Are you speaking and acting from a place of deep connection with Him, or are you trying to operate in authority without intimacy?

5. **"Worship often begins when we encounter more than we expected."** The disciples moved from "Will we survive?" to "Who is this man?" What question is God inviting you to shift from survival-focused to wonder-focused?

6. **"The calm stayed with the disciples and slowly changed how they understood Jesus."** What new understanding of Jesus is God developing in you through your current circumstances? How is your view of Him being refined?

PRACTICE:

- **Worship from wonder:** This week, set aside time to simply sit in silence and reflect on one aspect of Jesus' character that your recent storm has revealed. Don't rush to petition or problem-solving. Just let wonder lead you into worship. Write down what shifts in your heart when you worship from a place of awe rather than need.

CHAPTER 7

THE OTHER SIDE

***Every storm has a destination. Faith always lands
somewhere purposeful.***

*"When Jesus climbed out of the boat, a man possessed by an evil spirit
came out from the tombs to meet him." (Mark 5:2)*

———

THE STORM WAS OVER, AND THEY HAD REACHED THE OTHER
side. The disciples stepped out of the boat soaked and bewil-
dered, their legs still shaking from hours of fighting the wind
and waves.

They had survived, but something didn't feel right. Hills
rose from the beach, dotted with caves that served as tombs.
The isolation of the Gerasenes felt almost as frightening as
the storm they'd just escaped.

But Jesus did not hesitate. He stepped out of the boat and

walked up the beach as if He had been planning this all along. He knew exactly where He was and why He was there. The disciples followed, still trying to process what they'd just seen Jesus do to the wind and waves.

That's when they heard it. A scream from the hills. Raw and tortured. The kind of sound that comes from pain left alone for too long. They froze on the shoreline. Jesus kept walking.

A figure stumbled down from among the tombs. His movements were erratic, as if his body no longer belonged to him. His skin was scarred and bloodied from wounds he'd inflicted on himself. Broken chains hung from his wrists and ankles—evidence that someone had tried to restrain him and failed. He wore nothing. He lived among the dead.

The disciples stood frozen on the sand as Jesus walked straight toward him. And that was when it began to make sense.

Back at the start of the journey, Jesus had said, *"Let us go over to the other side."* (Mark 4:35) He hadn't explained why. Now the meaning of those words stood in front of them.

The crossing hadn't been accidental. The storm had been purposeful. Every moment they were sure they were going to die had carried them here, to this man.

During the storm, they'd shouted at Jesus, asking if He cared that they were dying. Now they had their answer. It stood before them, scarred and bound, waiting on the shore.

Yes, He cared. Just not in the way they'd expected.

———

THE MAN NO ONE COULD HELP

Mark doesn't soften the details of what Jesus and the disciples found on the shore of the Gerasenes.

"This man lived in the burial caves and could no longer be restrained, even with a chain. Whenever he was put into chains and shackles—and he often was—he snapped the chains from his wrists and slashed the shackles. No one was strong enough to subdue him. Day and night he wandered among the burial caves and in the hills, howling and cutting himself with sharp stones."[1]

Can I encourage you to read that again slowly?

This man didn't just have occasional struggles. Day and night, he wandered, howled, and cut himself. His community had tried everything to help him and had failed. They had bound him with chains, the strongest restraints they had. He broke them. They tried iron shackles. He snapped those too. They attempted to subdue him with force. He overpowered them.

Eventually, they stopped trying.

That's what happens when nothing works. When every attempt to help someone fails, people give up. They don't mean to be cruel. They just become exhausted. They run out of options and out of hope. So they let him live among the dead.

The Greek word Mark uses for "tombs" is *mnēmeion*, which literally means a place of memory, a memorial.[2] Don't miss the irony of where he was living. Tombs exist to remember the dead, but this man had been forgotten by the living. He existed in the space between life and death, remembered by no one, surrounded by monuments of people who had once mattered to someone.

He spent his nights howling in the darkness and his days cutting himself with stones. No one came to check on him any longer. The community had drawn a line of separation. They, the living, stayed on one side of the line, and he remained with the dead.

Think about what that does to a person. The isolation. The abandonment. The daily confirmation that you are too broken for anyone to fix, too dangerous for anyone to love, too far gone for anyone to reach.

He was breathing, but he'd been buried alive.

Don't forget that someone once loved this man. He was someone's son. Someone's brother. Perhaps before the demons came, he'd had friends.

But now? Now he was just the man in the tombs. The one people warned their children to stay away from. The one everyone had decided was beyond help.

I wonder how many people walked past those tombs and heard his screams. How many had considered helping him but then kept walking because they'd decided it was too risky, too hard, or even hopeless?

The community's verdict was clear: He's too far gone.

Damon West knows what it feels like to be too far gone. He was a college football quarterback with a promising future. Then, his addiction to methamphetamine destroyed everything. Within a few years, he was running one of the largest burglary and theft rings in North Texas history. When police finally caught him, he was sentenced to 65 years in a maximum-security prison.

Sixty-five years. The message was clear: He would die in prison.

Damon became exactly what the system expected. He became angry, violent, and survived prison life by intimidation. He was stabbed multiple times. He stabbed others. He spent time in solitary confinement. The guards knew him.

The inmates feared him. Everyone agreed: This is who Damon West is now. A career criminal. A lost cause.

However, in 2009, something shifted. A prison volunteer looked past the hopelessness of Damon's condition and saw something else. He believed Damon could still be reached. That volunteer introduced Damon to Jesus. And slowly, in one of the darkest places in America, Damon surrendered his life to Jesus, and he began to change.

He started mentoring younger inmates instead of exploiting them. He earned two master's degrees while incarcerated. He became known, not for violence, but for the message of hope he shared with his fellow inmates.

Then, in 2014, after seven years from the day he became a prisoner, the unimaginable happened. Damon was paroled and released from prison. Not because the sentence changed, but because the man did. His sentence was commuted due to the transformation everyone witnessed.

Today, Damon West speaks to hundreds of thousands of people each year about redemption. He co-wrote *The Coffee Bean* with Jon Gordon, a book that's sold over a million copies. He's a husband, a father, and a living example that no one is too far gone for God to reach.[3]

The man the system wrote off became the man God wrote into a new story. The words of Tim Keller remind us of the redemptive power of Jesus: *"The gospel is this: We are more sinful and flawed in ourselves than we ever dared believe, yet at the very same time we are more loved and accepted in Jesus Christ than we ever dared hope."*[4]

Damon West represents both halves of that truth. In prison, facing 65 years, he embodied the first half as living proof that some situations look absolutely hopeless. But he became living proof of the second half. Jesus reaches people in places the rest of us won't go.

The demoniac also represented this same gospel truth.

———

WHAT THE CHAINS COULDN'T DO

The chains had failed. Not because they weren't strong enough, but because chains can only restrain a body. They can't touch what's tormenting a soul.

His community had made an error. They made the same mistake the disciples had made, thinking the storm was a natural phenomenon. The community thought they were dealing with a behavior problem. Jesus knew they were dealing with a spiritual issue. They tried to contain him. Jesus came to free him.

This matters because we make the same mistake. We try to manage what needs to be delivered, modify what needs to be transformed, when what we really need is to surrender to the only One who has authority over it.

How many of us are trying to change behaviors when what we need is freedom from the source behind them? How many are attempting to restrain habits or manage addictions that keep snapping back no matter how strong our resolve?

The demoniac's broken chains should tell us something: Our willpower isn't the answer. Our strategies aren't enough. Our best attempts at self-control will eventually fail if we're fighting on the wrong level.

Jesus didn't come with stronger chains. He came with a stronger Word. And He was about to speak it to the one person everyone else had given up on.

WHY THIS PLACE?

The desperation of this lonely man is magnified by the isolation of the location. Geography matters in this story.

Jesus didn't accidentally end up in the region of the Gerasenes. He had commanded His disciples to cross the lake. *"Let us go over to the other side."*[5] The initial command to start this adventure was intentional. He didn't say, "Let's get on the boat and see where the wind takes us." Or, "Let's set sail, and we'll figure it out when we get there." He had a destination in mind.

That destination was as far from ideal as you could get. Gerasa was in a pagan country and quite different from Jesus' normal destination. No crowds were waiting to hear His wisdom. When He stepped onto the shoreline, no religious leaders rushed out to debate Old Testament laws with Him. There were just tombs in the hillside and a coastline that smelled like death.

The other side wasn't on any ministry roadmap.

Mark makes sure we understand the isolation. One man. One demon-possessed man, living in one of the most remote and forgotten corners of an unlikely region. There would not be hundreds of people gathering to hear Jesus speak. There wasn't going to be a revival breaking out in Gerasa. There was just this one broken man that no one wanted to deal with.

Think about the logic of it. Jesus had just spent days teaching massive crowds gathered on the opposite shore. Miracles were happening as people were being healed. His ministry was exploding. The momentum was building.

And He left.

He told His disciples to get in the boat and row away from

the crowds, away from the success, and away from the people who wanted more of Him. He rowed toward a place where nobody wanted Him at all.

Why?

For one man.

The Greek word Mark uses earlier in verse 1 is *eis*, which means *into or unto*, *indicating direction and purpose*.[6] Jesus went *unto* the other side. This wasn't a casual trip. This wasn't Plan B when Plan A fell through. This was intentional and planned.

From a strategic perspective, this trip made little sense. You don't leave the crowds to go where there are no crowds, nor abandon momentum to go where there's no movement. You don't risk your disciples' lives crossing a dangerous lake in the middle of the night to reach one person in a cemetery.

Unless that one person is the whole point.

You don't risk your disciples' lives crossing a dangerous lake in the middle of the night to reach one person in a cemetery.

The community had decided the demoniac's future: suppose he's never set free?

But Jesus came with a different question: Suppose he is set free?

In the classic Winnie the Pooh story, Eeyore loses his tail. His friends search everywhere but can't find it. Christopher Robin visits Eeyore in his gloomy place and asks, "What would you do if your tail came back?"

Eeyore replies with characteristic pessimism: "But it won't."

Christopher Robin persists gently: "But supposing it did?"[7]

That small shift—from "it won't" to "supposing it did"—changes everything. It's the difference between resignation and hope. Between writing someone off and believing restoration is possible. Between assuming the worst and daring to imagine redemption.

The community looked at the demoniac and asked, "What if he never changes?"

Jesus looked at him and asked, "What if he does?"

That's still the question Jesus asks about the people we've given up on. The addicts. Those who are angry. People who are isolated. The ones living in their tombs. While we're deciding who's too far gone, Jesus is crossing storms to prove we're wrong.

———

THE PLACE NO ONE GOES

We have modern tombs too. Places in every community that people avoid. Neighborhoods you warn your kids about. Communities where the forgotten live. We just don't call them tombs.

Unfortunately, we do what that first-century community did. We let people live there because we don't know what else to do with them. It's not that we haven't tried; it's just that we're out of options. Therefore, we draw lines and remain on our side, while they remain on theirs.

However, Jesus crossed the lines. He always has. He touched lepers when everyone else kept their distance. He ate with tax collectors when everyone else refused to share a table with them. He spoke to a Samaritan woman whom everyone else avoided because of her adultery.

Now, in the middle of the night, He rode through a storm that nearly killed everyone onboard to walk a beach in pagan territory. Why? Because there was one man that everyone else had decided wasn't worth the effort.

It certainly wasn't ministry strategy. But it was love. The kind of love that goes where no one else will go. To the one person everyone else has abandoned.

———

ARE YOU THE FORGOTTEN ONE?

Maybe you see yourself in this man. Not the demons or the chains necessarily, but the isolation. The sense that you've tried everything and nothing's worked. You are exhausted from fighting battles no one else can see. The growing suspicion that you're the one person who's just too broken, too complicated, too far gone has become overwhelming

Maybe people have tried to help you. They meant well. They prayed for you. They gave you advice. They offered solutions that worked for everyone else but somehow didn't work for you. And then, without saying it verbally, you felt them stepping back. You knew it wasn't because they stopped caring. They had simply run out of answers.

So you stopped asking, and you learned to manage alone. You started hiding your struggles. You began trying to convince everyone, including yourself, that you were fine even when you were barely holding on. You built your own tomb. Perhaps not carved in a hillside, but just as isolating and lonely.

And somewhere along the way, you started believing the lie that God helps other people but probably not you.

Here's what I need you to hear: Jesus didn't cross that lake for the man everyone remembered. He crossed it for the man everyone forgot.

He didn't come for the person who had it all together. He came for the one who'd broken every chain the community tried to use to help him. The one who lived in the place between life and death.

And today, that is still who Jesus risks storms to reach. Not the put-together people or the ones who've figured it out. Not the success stories with the impressive testimonies. He comes for the ones still living in the tombs, fighting battles in the dark. He pushes through to the ones who've stopped believing rescue is possible.

The demoniac didn't call out to Jesus. He didn't ask for help. He had no idea Jesus was coming. He was just surviving another day in his private torment, doing what he'd done for years—screaming, bleeding, and breaking.

Jesus came anyway.

That's the point. You don't have to have enough faith. Cleaning yourself up first or figuring out how to ask for help in the right way isn't a prerequisite. You don't even have to believe rescue is coming.

Jesus is already walking toward you. He approaches you in the same manner that He walked toward the beach in Gerasa. He comes to you with the same intentionality and determination. You can be assured that He will cross whatever distance, brave whatever storm, and enter whatever graveyard stands between Him and you.

Because you're not the exception. You're not too far gone. You're not the one case that's too complicated even for God.

You're the reason He got in the boat.

The storm the disciples survived? That was the cost of reaching you. The terror they felt? That was the price of your freedom. The night they thought they'd die? That was the route to your rescue.

You are not forgotten. You are not abandoned. You are not alone in your tomb.

You're the one He came to rescue.

———

What happened next on that beach would prove something the disciples were still learning. The storm hadn't been a mistake. The terror hadn't been meaningless. The night they thought they'd die hadn't been wasted. Every wave that crashed over the bow, every moment they were certain they wouldn't make it. It all had a purpose.

It had brought them here. To this man. To this moment.

"God is not afraid of your mess. In fact, He's already planning to use it."[8] The demoniac's life was about as messy as it gets. There were broken chains, a broken mind, a broken body, and living among the dead. Jesus didn't see a mess. He saw a mission.

The man everyone had written off was the man Jesus had been writing in His plans all along. The forgotten man had actually never been forgotten. He'd just been waiting for the One who would cross any distance, brave any storm, and walk into any graveyard to bring him home.

Jesus walked up the beach toward the demoniac with the same calm He'd displayed when He stood up and spoke to the wind. The disciples probably stayed back. Can you blame them? They'd survived one storm, and they weren't eager to walk into another.

But Jesus moved forward.

Storms don't intimidate the One who calms them, and demons don't frighten the One who commands them. Broken people don't scare off the One who has come specifically to make them whole.

Storms don't intimidate the One who calms them, and demons don't frighten the One who commands them. Broken people don't scare off the One who has come specifically to make them whole.

The man everyone had given up on was about to discover what the disciples had learned during the crossing. When Jesus decides you're worth reaching, nothing can stop Him from getting to you.

Not distance. Not danger. Not even death itself. The question wasn't whether He could save this man. The question was why He would risk everything to do it.

———

REFLECT:

1. **"Every storm has a destination. Faith always lands somewhere purposeful."** Looking back at a storm you've already come through, what "other side" did God bring you to that you wouldn't

have reached any other way? What or who was waiting there?

2. **The demoniac was "too broken for anyone to fix, too dangerous for anyone to love, too far gone for anyone to reach."** Have you ever felt that way about yourself? Or is there someone in your life you've privately decided is "too far gone"? How does this story challenge that belief?

3. **"Chains can only restrain a body. They can't touch what's tormenting a soul."** What "chains" have you been relying on to manage a deeper issue (willpower, accountability, programs, strategies)? What would it look like to let Jesus address the spiritual root instead of just managing symptoms?

4. **Jesus left crowds and momentum to reach one forgotten man.** Who is the "one" God might be asking you to notice, reach out to, or invest in— even if it doesn't make strategic sense? What's holding you back?

5. **"You don't have to have enough faith. You don't even have to believe rescue is coming. Jesus is already walking toward you."** What burden of "getting it right" do you need to release? Where have you been trying to qualify yourself for Jesus' help instead of simply receiving it?

6. **The chapter ends with: "You're the reason He got in the boat."** Let that truth sink in. Does it feel true to you, or do doubt rise up? Talk to God honestly about which one you feel and why.

PRACTICE:

Identify your tomb:

- Where have you been living in isolation, convinced freedom isn't possible? Write it down.
- Then write this truth under it: "Jesus crossed a storm to reach me here."
- This week, take one small step toward freedom—tell one trusted person about your struggle, reach out for help, or speak one truth out loud that counters the lie you've been believing.

CHAPTER 8

THE ONE WORTH
EVERYTHING

His Power Takes Us From Torment To Testimony

"When Jesus was still some distance away, the man saw him, ran to meet him, and bowed low before him. With a shriek, he screamed, 'Why are you interfering with me, Jesus, Son of the Most High God? In the name of God, I beg you, don't torture me!'" (Mark 5:6-7)

———

SOME PEOPLE ARE WORTH CROSSING OCEANS TO VISIT. THIS man was worth confronting hell in order to bring deliverance.

The disciples stood frozen on the beach, watching their Rabbi walk toward a man who looked more like a monster than a human. Chains hung from his wrists, and blood covered his body. And then the man saw Jesus and ran straight at Him.

Everything in the disciples screamed for them to get back in the boat.

But Jesus didn't hesitate. He walked straight to the man everyone else had run from.

Perhaps now they were beginning to understand something that could redefine everything they thought they knew about God. The storm had not been about getting to the other side. It had been about getting to this one man.

In the boat, they had screamed at Jesus: *"Teacher, don't You care that we're going to drown?"*[1] Now, as Jesus walked toward the demoniac, they saw the answer.

Yes, He cared. He cared so much that it appeared He had risked thirteen lives to save one. That's not the math the world uses. But it's the math of heaven.

In God's economy, one lost soul is worth any cost.[2] And one demon-possessed man living in a graveyard was worth sailing through a storm to reach.

Jesus wasn't doing the math. He was showing love.

———

THE ENCOUNTER

As Jesus approached the man, everything escalated. The demoniac saw Him coming and ran straight at Him—not away, but toward Him. Mark describes it as the man running from a distance, and when he reached Jesus, he fell on his knees.[3]

It's a strange detail. This man had overpowered everyone who'd tried to restrain him. He'd snapped chains and broken iron shackles. He was stronger than multiple men combined. And yet when he got to Jesus, he collapsed at His feet. Something in him recognized authority.

Then he screamed. *"What do you want with me, Jesus, Son of the Most High God? In God's name don't torture me!"*[4]

Stop and think about what just happened. The demons possessing this man knew exactly who Jesus was. They called Him by name. They identified Him as the Son of the Most High God. They even begged Him not to torture them.

The disciples had just spent hours in a boat with Jesus, watching Him sleep through a storm before He stood up and commanded the wind and waves to stop. They'd asked, *"Who is this? Even the wind and waves obey Him!"*[5] On the shore, even though they were in awe of His power, they were still trying to figure out who Jesus was.

The demons already knew.

Mark tells us that Jesus said to the evil spirit, *"Come out of this man!"*[6] This wasn't a long exorcism. Jesus didn't need rituals, formulas, or backup plans. He spoke, and the demons had to respond—but they tried to negotiate.

Jesus asked a question: "What is your name?"

"My name is Legion," the demon answered, "for we are many."[7]

The Greek word *legiōn* is a transliteration from the Latin *legio*—the Roman military unit that occupied and oppressed the Jewish people.[8] A Roman legion consisted of up to 6,000 soldiers. The word "Legion" carried brutal associations of Roman legions that had destroyed villages, crucified rebels, and represented foreign domination.

Can you see the irony in this encounter? This man living, in Gentile territory, was occupied by forces that identified themselves with the language of Rome's military oppression. He was possessed by an army, and he'd been losing the war for years.

> **This man living, in Gentile territory, was occupied by forces that identified themselves with the language of Rome's military oppression. He was possessed by an army, and he'd been losing the war for years.**

No wonder the chains hadn't worked and people had given up on him. It's obvious why he had been living in the tombs, screaming through the nights, and cutting himself with stones. He wasn't just possessed. His soul was a spiritual battlefield.

The demons begged Jesus repeatedly not to send them out of the area.[9] Think about that. They knew they had to leave the man. That wasn't up for debate. Jesus had already decided. But they were trying to bargain over where they'd go next.

Even in their desperation, they recognized Jesus' absolute authority over them.

Then they saw the pigs. A large herd was feeding on a nearby hillside. The evil spirits made their request: *"Send us among the pigs; allow us to go into them."*[10]

Jesus gave them permission. One word was all it took. The demons left the man and entered the pigs. The entire herd—about two thousand of them—rushed down the steep bank into the lake and drowned.[11]

"When Jesus cast out demons, he was doing what no amount of religious reform could accomplish. He was defeating, in person-to-person combat, the powers that had kept Israel and the world in bondage."[12]

That's what the disciples were witnessing. Not just a miracle. A declaration of war. Jesus was defeating the forces of hell in direct combat, demonstrating that the kingdom of God had arrived with power.

That's what the disciples were witnessing. Not just a miracle. A declaration of war. Jesus defeated the forces of hell, one person at a time, demonstrating that the kingdom of God had arrived with power.

The transformation was immediate. The man they'd been afraid of was suddenly still. The screaming stopped. The violence ended. In an instant, the demons that had tormented him for years vanished.

Jesus hadn't touched him. He hadn't performed elaborate rituals. He did not need time to prepare, nor did he need reinforcements. He simply spoke, and it was done.

The voice that had calmed the storm had just freed a man from an army of demons. The disciples were learning something they'd need for the rest of their ministry: when Jesus speaks, everything, wind, waves, demons, death itself, has to obey.

———

SITTING CLOTHED AND IN HIS RIGHT MIND

Word spread quickly. The people who'd been tending the pigs ran, sprinted into the town and countryside, and told everyone what had happened. Then the crowd came.[13]

They came to see the spectacle. Maybe they expected to find the demoniac still raging among the tombs. Perhaps they wanted to see the destroyed pig herd for themselves. Maybe they were just curious about the Rabbi they'd heard so much about. What they found stopped them cold.

"When they came to Jesus, they saw the man who had been

possessed by the legion of demons, sitting there, dressed and in his right mind; and they were afraid."[14]

Sitting. Dressed. In his right mind.

What they saw tells you everything about the transformation. The man who'd been running wild through the tombs was sitting calmly. The man who'd been naked was now clothed. The man who'd been tormented was thinking clearly for the first time in years.

Mark wants us to see the contrast. This wasn't a partial improvement. He wasn't testifying, "I'm better, but still struggling." This was complete restoration. The man who'd been living like an animal among the tombs was suddenly, fully himself again.

However, the people didn't celebrate. They weren't even relieved. They were terrified. You'd think they'd be thankful. For years, this man had been a nightmare for the town. Parents kept their kids away from the tombs because of him. He had been the one screaming every night, the one no shackles could hold, and the one everyone had given up on.

Now he was free, healed, and restored.

Unbelievably, their response was fear. Those who had seen it happen told the others how Jesus had healed the man. They described the demons, the pigs rushing into the lake, everything.[15] But the explanation didn't bring comfort. It brought more fear, because power like that is unsettling.

When you see someone perform actions that seem impossible and witness their authority over uncontrollable forces, you're compelled to make a decision. Either you surrender to that power, or you push it away.

The people of the Gerasenes made their choice. *"Then all the people of the region of the Gerasenes asked Jesus to leave them, because they were overcome with fear."*[16]

They asked Him to leave. The One who had just freed their most tormented neighbor. The One who had demonstrated power over the spiritual forces that had devastated one of their own. They looked at Jesus and said, "Please go."

They chose the familiar over the freedom Jesus offered.

It's easier to live with familiar brokenness than to face the One who can actually fix it. If He can heal that man, He might also ask something of us. If He has authority over demons, He might have authority over us, too. Of course, some people would rather stay in their tombs than surrender to the One who can lead them out.

It's easier to live with familiar brokenness than to face the One who can actually fix it.

The man who had been delivered saw it differently.

"As Jesus was getting into the boat, the man who had been demon-possessed begged to go with him."[17]

Of course he did. Jesus had given him his life back. He'd freed him from years of torment. He'd restored his humanity. Where else would he want to be except close to the One who'd saved him?

But Jesus said no. *"Go home to your own people and tell them how much the Lord has done for you, and how he has had mercy on you."*[18]

Go home. Go back to the people who'd chained you. Go back to the community that had given up on you. Go back to the place where everyone knows what you were. Tell them what happened.

That's not the assignment the man wanted. But it was the

assignment he needed. Jesus wasn't saying no to him. He was giving him a commission.

"So the man went away and began to tell in the Decapolis how much Jesus had done for him. And all the people were amazed."[19]

The people who had been afraid of Jesus now had to deal with the continual testimony of the man who was healed. The people of Gerasa could reject the Deliverer, but they could not deny the deliverance. They would see and hear the evidence every day, walking in their community, clothed and in his right mind.

Sometimes the most powerful sermon isn't the one preached from behind a pulpit. It's the one lived by the person everyone said was too far gone.

Shirlene and I were in our first pastorate, and I was learning things they don't teach you in seminary. I knew how to conduct a business meeting, officiate a wedding, and visit hospitals. But there were other things—supernatural things— I was completely unprepared for.

During a revival service one evening, I was standing at the pulpit preparing to open the service when I saw the back door of the sanctuary open. A young man I had never seen before tucked his head inside for a moment. The look on his face was pure terror. He quickly pulled back.

A few minutes later, he returned with a couple from our church who had brought him. They took seats on the back row.

We sang a few songs. From the platform, I watched him. His fear was obvious. That's when the Holy Spirit spoke quietly: "He is oppressed by demons."

I need to be honest with you. While I don't doubt the reality of demonic oppression, I had never encountered it before that night, and it has seldom happened since. Even today, I rarely see demonic possession that I can easily identify. But I knew this situation was different.

I quietly went to the evangelist leading the revival and whispered what I had sensed. We called the church to prayer and walked to the back row. We asked the young man if we could pray for him.

He immediately fell to the floor and began thrashing as if having a seizure. But he was pleading: "Help me. Please help me."

I won't detail everything that happened during that time of prayer. But I will tell you this: at a certain point, the young man stopped convulsing. He looked up at us. He stood to his feet. And with a smile on his face, he whispered, "I'm free. It's gone."

The terror that had gripped him was gone. The oppression that had driven him was broken. He walked out of that church a different person than when he had entered.

I know some people don't believe in demonic oppression. But I was there. I know what happened. And I know what I saw in that young man's face when freedom came—the same thing the people of Gerasa saw when they looked at the man who had been living in the tombs.

Sitting. Clothed. In his right mind.

Jesus is still in the deliverance business.

———

WHAT ABOUT YOU?

The battle on the beach ends with two different responses to Jesus, and both of them matter. There's the man who was delivered. And there's the community that walked away.

Maybe you're the man sitting on the beach, finally free

after years of torment. You know what it's like to be bound by something you couldn't break on your own. You've tried to overcome it through your willpower, through strategies, by being accountable to others, or through self-help programs—and nothing worked. The chains kept snapping back.

Then Jesus spoke into your life, and everything changed.

If that's you, hear what Jesus said to the delivered man: "Go home and tell them what the Lord has done for you."

Your story isn't just for you. It's for the people who knew you when you were still in chains. It's for the ones who've given up hope that freedom is possible. It's for those sitting in their own tombs right now, convinced they're too far gone.

Your story isn't just for you. It's for the people who knew you when you were still in chains. It's for the ones who've given up hope that freedom is possible. It's for those sitting in their own tombs right now, convinced they're too far gone.

You don't need a theology degree to be a witness. You just need to be honest about what Jesus did. The man Jesus healed didn't plant a church or start a ministry. He simply went back to his region and told people what had happened. And Mark says all the people were amazed.[20]

Your transformed life is the testimony. Let people see it and ask questions. Let them wonder how someone who was that broken became this whole.

That's what Jesus meant when He said, "Go home." Not "stay quiet about this." Not "keep it private." Go home and live your freedom out loud.

Perhaps you are not the one who was delivered. Maybe you are part of the community standing on the beach, looking at the evidence of what Jesus can do and feeling... afraid.

Afraid of what it means if He's really that powerful. Perhaps you fear what He might ask if you let Him get too close. Afraid of surrendering control to someone whose authority is absolute.

The people of the Gerasenes looked at a transformed man and asked Jesus to leave. They chose the comfort of the familiar over the risk of encountering real power. They wanted their pigs more than they wanted the Deliverer.

Don't make that choice.

Yes, Jesus has authority over everything. Encountering Him means you can't stay the same. When you allow Him into your life, you surrender areas you've tried to control on your own.

Look at what He does with that authority. He uses it to free people and to restore what's been broken. He uses His authority to calm storms and restore those who have been marginalized.

The same authority that terrified the community was the power that saved the man. The tragedy of this story isn't just that the community rejected Jesus. It's what they missed. They could have had more healings. More people could have experienced deliverance. More people could have encountered the One who has authority over every force that destroys human life. Instead, they chose to stay exactly where they were.

———

We are all faced with the decision of what we will do with the One who is still walking onto beaches where broken people live. What we will do with the God who is still speaking freedom over those who have been tormented for years. He is still offering to do for you what no chain, no strategy, no human effort could accomplish.

The man on the beach didn't earn his deliverance. He didn't qualify for it. He didn't clean himself up first or figure out the right words to say.

Jesus just showed up and freed him.

That's still how it works.

———

REFLECT:

1. **"Some people are worth crossing oceans to visit. This man was worth confronting hell for."** Do you believe you are worth that much to Jesus? What makes it hard to accept that truth? What would change in your life if you fully believed it?

2. **"The demons recognized Jesus immediately, but the disciples were still figuring out who He was."** What keeps you from recognizing Jesus' authority in your current situation? What would help you see Him more clearly?

3. **"The transformation was complete and immediate—'sitting, clothed, and in his right mind'."** What area of your life are you settling for "better but still struggling" when Jesus offers

complete restoration? What keeps you from believing complete freedom is possible?

4. **"The community chose fear over faith and asked Jesus to leave."** Have you ever resisted God's work because it felt too disruptive, too costly, or too uncomfortable? What did you miss by choosing the familiar over His freedom?

5. **"Jesus told the delivered man, 'Go home and tell them'."** If Jesus has brought breakthrough, healing, or freedom in your life, who needs to hear your story? What's keeping you from sharing it?

6. **This chapter offers two applications: Are you the delivered one, or the fearful community?** Which one do you identify with most right now? What is Jesus specifically inviting you to do in response?

PRACTICE:

There is a two-part response:

- If you're the delivered one: Write down your "go home and tell them" assignment. Who specifically needs to hear what Jesus has done for you? Make a plan this week to share your testimony with at least one person—not a polished sermon, just the honest truth about the freedom Jesus has brought you.
- If you're the fearful community: Identify what you're afraid of surrendering to Jesus. Write it down. Then ask Him: "What am I afraid I'll lose if I let You have full authority here?" Listen for His answer. What might you actually gain?

CHAPTER 9

CONCLUSION

I BEGAN THIS BOOK WITH A MEMORY OF AN OKLAHOMA SKY turning green, and a child's fear of what was coming. I've spent my life learning what I didn't know that day: the storm doesn't get the final word. Jesus does.

The disciples climbed back into the boat, their minds still processing what they'd just witnessed. They'd crossed a lake through a storm that nearly killed them. They were convinced they couldn't survive. The terror and exhaustion had been overwhelming. The certainty they were going to die was as real as the storm itself.

Then, they watched Jesus walk toward a man possessed by an army of demons. They saw the confrontation. They watched with continued awe as the man was delivered. There was no denying the transformation. With amazement, they witnessed a community choose fear over faith and a delivered man choose testimony over comfort.

Now they were heading back across the water, leaving behind a man who'd never be the same.

Standing on that beach, watching a man sit clothed and in his right mind, they'd learned something about the heart of God they'd never forget.

One person is worth it. Worth the risk. Worth the storm. Worth the journey into territory where no one else would go. Jesus had proven it by going.

What the disciples didn't know yet was that this pattern would define the rest of their lives. They would follow Jesus into forgotten places for forgotten people. Following their Rabbi meant they would keep crossing lines no one else would cross. They would have more opportunities to join Him using Heaven's authority and power to restore what the Enemy had broken.

He is still inviting us to come along. Because the Kingdom of God isn't built in comfortable places by comfortable people. He invites us to take the Kingdom into the tombs and the storms of our lives, to our generation, to our location. He continues to call us to the places where only Divine power can make a difference.

The Kingdom of God isn't built in comfortable places by comfortable people. He invites us to take the Kingdom into the tombs and the storms of our lives, to our generation, to our location.

The other side wasn't the destination. It was the mission field. And there are always more people waiting on the other side.

YOUR OTHER SIDE

You may have an "other side" in your life right now. That place you don't want to go. A storm you don't want to face. An individual you'd rather avoid. A situation that feels too hard, too risky, and too far beyond what you think you can handle.

Maybe it's a relationship that needs reconciliation, but the conversation terrifies you. Perhaps it's a calling you've been running from because it would cost you everything comfortable. Is there a person in your life who seems too broken, too far gone, too much work?

Maybe it's your own tomb—that place where you've been living in isolation, convinced that freedom isn't possible for someone like you.

Whatever your "other side" is, Jesus is saying the same thing He said to those disciples two thousand years ago: "Let us go over to the other side."

He didn't say, "Let Me go while you stay safe here." Nor, "Wait until conditions are better." And certainly not, "Come when you feel ready."

Let us go. Together. Now.

He invites you into the storm because someone on the other side needs what only He can give. Or maybe you're the one on the other side who needs to be reached. Either way, the crossing matters.

The storm you are facing right now may be the route to your destiny, not the obstacle. The terror you feel may be the cost of getting to the deliverance God has planned. The night you think will destroy you might be the very thing that brings you to the place where only God can work.

Here is what the disciples learned that night: the storm revealed who Jesus was in ways the calm never could. When the winds are howling and the waves are crashing, that's when you discover that the One in the boat with you has authority over everything trying to destroy you. That's when you learn that His "Peace, be still" is stronger than any force of hell that's been unleashed against you.

And when you reach the other side, you may be exhausted and shaken, but you will discover that the crossing was worth it. Because there's a person who needs Jesus, or there's a version of yourself that can only be found on the far shore.

———

THE INVITATION STILL STANDS

We started with a storm and a question: "Teacher, don't You care that we're perishing?"

The answer to that question has been unfolding through every chapter. Yes, He cares. He cares so much that He'll risk everything to reach you. He calms the storm when you need rescuing and sustains you through it when you need to grow. He cares enough to take you places you'd never go on your own because there are people there who need what He can do through you.

Or perhaps you are the person He came to reach.

You are the one in the tombs. You scream through the night, trying to break chains that won't budge. Forgotten and abandoned, everyone has written you off as too far gone.

The good news is Jesus has already made the crossing. He's standing on your shore now, right in the middle of your desperation. He's not there with condemnation or disappointment. He doesn't come with a list of requirements you need to meet before He'll help you.

He's walking toward you with the same authority that calmed the storm and cast out the Legion. The same Power that spoke the universe into existence is speaking freedom over your life. The same Grace that reached a demon-possessed man in a Gentile graveyard is reaching toward you, wherever you are, whatever you've done, however long you've been bound.

The same Grace that reached a demon-possessed man in a Gentile graveyard is reaching toward you, wherever you are, whatever you've done, however long you've been bound.

You don't have to clean yourself up first. You don't have to wait until you have enough faith, courage, or strength.

Jesus is already on His way to you. He's already decided you're worth the journey. He's already chosen to cross whatever distance, brave whatever storm, and walk into whatever darkness that stands between Him and you.

The only question is whether you'll let Him reach you.

———

REFLECT:

1. **"One person is worth it. Worth the risk. Worth the storm. Worth the journey."** How does this truth reframe a difficult season you've walked through? Who was the "one" (including possibly yourself) that made the journey worth it?

2. **"The other side wasn't the destination. It was the mission field."** What if your breakthrough wasn't just for you, but for someone else who needs to see that freedom is possible? How does that shift your perspective on what you've been through?

3. **"You have an 'other side' in your life right now."** What is it? That place you don't want to go, the storm you don't want to face, the person you'd rather avoid, or the tomb you've been living in?

4. **"Jesus says, 'Let us go to the other side'—not 'Let Me go while you stay safe'."** What would it look like to stop waiting for perfect conditions and instead, trust that Jesus is with you in the crossing?

5. **"The storm you're facing right now may be the route to your destiny, not the obstacle."** If you believed that was true about your current difficulty, how would it change the way you pray, the way you persevere, or the way you view what's happening?

6. **"The book began with 'Teacher, don't You care that we're perishing?' and ends with Jesus standing on your shore."** How would you answer that question now, after walking through this journey? How has your understanding of God's care changed or deepened?

PRACTICE:
Your "other side" action plan:

- Name it: Write down the specific "other side" Jesus is calling you toward right now.

- Identify the fear: What are you most afraid will happen if you obey and get in the boat?
- Remember His faithfulness: List 2-3 times God has proven Himself faithful in past storms.
- Take one step: What is one concrete action you can take this week toward your "other side"? (Make the call, have the conversation, apply for the thing, forgive the person, get help, etc.)
- Invite Him: Pray this simple prayer: "Jesus, let us go to the other side. I'm getting in the boat. You lead. I'll follow."

YOUR FINAL
PERSONAL INVENTORY

Now that you have completed *"The Other Side: Finding Peace In The Middle Of Your Storm,"* take time to answer these overarching questions:

1. What was the most significant insight or truth God showed you through this journey?
2. How has your understanding of Jesus' character changed?
3. What specific fear, doubt, or belief about God has been challenged or transformed?
4. What is the one thing you need to do in response to what you've learned?
5. Who needs to hear what God has taught you through this book?
6. Six months from now, how do you hope this book will have changed your life?

NOTES

INTRODUCTION

1. Mark 4:38
2. Mark 4:39
3. Mark 4:41
4. 2 Timothy 4:6
5. *analýō*. Strong's Greek 360," BibleHub, https://biblehub.com/greek/360.htm.

1. THE CALM BEFORE CHAOS

1. Mark 4:1
2. Mark 4:35
3. Eugene H. Peterson. 1980. A Long Obedience in the Same Direction: Discipleship in an Instant Society, p. 165. Downers Grove, IL: InterVarsity Press
4. Genesis 12:1
5. Luke 5:4
6. Luke 5:5
7. "Biker Paid for the Stranger's Groceries Then Followed Her Home and She Called 911," Bikers Byte. https://bikersbyte.com/biker-paid-for-the-strangers-groceries-then-followed-her-home-and-she-called-911/
8. Philippians 2:13
9. Christine Caine, "Part of the Solution," Daily Email Devotional, November 1, 2025
10. *tehōm*. Strong's Hebrew 8415, BibleHub, https://biblehub.com/hebrew/8415.htm
11. Psalms 89:9
12. Branham, William M. 2017. An Exposition of the Seven Church Ages. Elizabethton, TN: Believers International
13. James 1:2–3
14. Tate, Albert. 2023. Disobedient God: Trusting a God Who Goes Off-Script, p. 146. New York: Faith Words
15. Nahum 1:3
16. Mark 4:36
17. Tiegreen, Chris. 2015. Dancing in the Desert Devotional Bible. Carol Stream, IL: Tyndale House Publishers
18. Luke 1:38

2. WHEN THE SKY TURNS BLACK

1. Hussain, Zoe, June 22, 2025. "6 Dead, 2 Missing after Boat Capsizes on Lake Tahoe." New York Post. https://nypost.com/2025/06/22/us-news/6-dead-2-missing-after-boat-caps
2. Mark 4:37 (KJV)
3. Mark 4:37
4. Renner, Rick. 2019. The Miracles of Jesus Christ, p. 65. Rick Renner Ministries: Tulsa, OK
5. John 10:10
6. Batterson, Mark. All In: You Are One Decision Away from a Totally Different Life, p. 87. Grand Rapids, MI: Zondervan, 2013
7. 1 Corinthians 16:9, KJV
8. Ephesians 2:2, KJV
9. Ephesians 6:12, KJV
10. Wolf, Katherine and Jay. Hope Heals: A True Story of Overwhelming Loss and an Overwhelming Love, pp. 163–165. Grand Rapids: Zondervan, 2016
11. Isaiah 54:17, KJV

3. PANIC IN THE BOAT

1. Eclov, Lee. Shepherding the Shepherd, p. 82. Christianity Today/Preaching Today Resources, 2021
2. Psalm 55:4-5
3. Mark 4:38
4. Matthew 10:29-31
5. Whittle, Daniel W. 1883. "I Know Whom I Have Believed." In *Gospel Hymns No. 4*, edited by Ira D. Sankey, James McGranahan, and George C. Stebbins. New York: Biglow & Main
6. 2 Timothy 1:12, KJV
7. Galatians 4:4
8. Mark 4:40

4. THE SLEEPING SAVIOR

1. Yamada, Haley. January 25, 2023. *Flight attendant goes viral for helping nervous passenger.* ABC News. https://abcnews.go.com/GMA/Living/flight-attendant-viral-helping-nervous-passenger/story?id=96667343
2. Matthew 11:28
3. "Anapauó." Strong's Concordance. BibleHub. https://biblehub.com/greek/373.htm

4. The History of The Pause That Refreshes Campaign. History Oasis. June 5, 2023. https://www.historyoasis.com/post/the-pause-that-refreshes-campaign
5. Philemon 7
6. *Airō*, Strong's Concordance, BibleHub, https://biblehub.com/greek/142.htm
7. *Zugos*, Strong's Concordance, BibleHub, https://biblehub.com/greek/2218.htm
8. Hebrews 6:19
9. Schell, Andy. "The Lost Art of Kedging: How to Set a Kedge Anchor." SAIL Magazine, May 31, 2013. https://sailmagazine.com/cruising/the-lost-art-of-kedging-how-to-set-a-kedge-anchor/
10. Hebrews 6:19
11. Miles, Charles A. 1906. "I've Anchored in Jesus."
12. Mark 4:38
13. *proskephalaion*. Strong's Greek 4344. BibleHub. https://biblehub.com/greek/4344.htm
14. Groeschel, Craig. The Benefit of Doubt: How Confronting Your Deepest Questions Can Lead to a Richer Faith. Grand Rapids, MI: Zondervan, 2025
15. Matthew 28:17
16. John 20:25
17. Hebrews 12:1-2
18. Psalm 23:4

5. THE VOICE THAT STILLED THE WIND

1. *epitimaō*. Strong's Greek 2008, BibleHub, https://biblehub.com/greek/2008.htm
2. Renner, Rick. 2019. The Miracles of Jesus, p. 65. Tulsa, OK: Rick Renner Ministries
3. Mark 4:39
4. *phimōthēti*. Strong's Greek 5392,d BibleHub, https://biblehub.com/greek/5392.htm
5. Luke 4:35
6. Renner, p. 66
7. Sullenberger, Chesley, and Jeffrey Zaslow. 2009. Highest Duty: My Search for What Really Matters, pp. 207-225. New York: William Morrow
8. Psalm 33:9, ESV
9. Ephesians 6:12
10. Batterson, Mark. 2016. Chase The Lion: If Your Dream Doesn't Scare You, It's Too Small. Colorado Springs, CO: Multinomah
11. Mark 4:39

6. GREAT STORM — GREATER CALM

1. Mark 4:39, KJV
2. Caine, Christine. 2017. Unshakeable, p. 77. Grand Rapids, MI: Zondervan
3. Exodus 14
4. Judges 6
5. John 5:19; 8:28; 12:49
6. Mark 4:41
7. Jonah 1:16

7. THE OTHER SIDE

1. Mark 5:3-5
2. *Mnēmeion*, Strong's Greek 3419, BibleHub, https://biblehub.com/greek/3419.htm
3. West, Damon, and Jon Gordon. 2019. The Coffee Bean: A Simple Lesson to Create Positive Change. Hoboken, NJ: Wiley
4. Keller, Timothy. 2008. The Prodigal God, p. 90. New York: Penguin Books
5. Mark 4:35
6. *Eis*. Strong's Greek 1519, BibleHub, https://biblehub.com/greek/1519.htm
7. Milne, A.A. 1926. Winnie-the-Pooh. London: Methuen & Co. Ltd.
8. Giglio, Louie. 2017. Goliath Must Fall, p. 23. Nashville, TN: W Publishing Group

8. THE ONE WORTH EVERYTHING

1. Mark 4:38
2. The three parables in Luke 15 demonstrates God's compassion for one: one sheep, one coin, one son.
3. Mark 5:6
4. Mark 5:7
5. Mark 4:41
6. Mark 5:8
7. Mark 5:9
8. *Legiōn*. Strong's Greek 3003, BibleHub, https://biblehub.com/greek/3003.htm
9. Mark 5:10
10. Mark 5:12
11. Mark 5:13
12. Wright, N.T. 1996. Jesus and the Victory of God, p. 193. Minneapolis: Fortress Press

13. Mark 5:14-15
14. Mark 5:15
15. Mark 5:16
16. Mark 5:17
17. Mark 5:18
18. Mark 5:19
19. Mark 5:20
20. Mark 5:20

SCRIPTURE INDEX

ABOUT THE AUTHOR

Duke and his wife, Shirlene, currently serve as the State Bishop for the Church of God of Prophecy in North Carolina. They served in a similar role in the Magnolia Region of Louisiana and Mississippi for six years. They have also served as National Evangelists for the International Offices of the Churches of God of Prophecy, and as pastors in Indiana, Florida, and Tennessee.

Duke has a Master of Education degree from the University of Tennessee. He was the founder and Head of School for Hamilton Heights Christian Academy, a fully accredited high school in Chattanooga, TN. During his tenure as the Head of School, Hamilton Heights served students from the greater Chattanooga area and over 180 students from 30 different nations across North America, South America, Europe, Asia, Australia, and Africa.

For over thirty years, Duke wrote high school and collegiate literature for the *One Accord* educational curriculum. He has authored two Bible studies for ***spiritmatters*** curriculum on the life of Moses and the life of Jonah.

Duke and Shirlene have three grown children: Michael and his wife, Ceren; Krystal and her husband, Jason; and Stephen and his wife, Caitlin. They have nine grandchildren, with the 10th expected in the spring of 2026!

instagram.com/dukestone1
facebook.com/duke.stone.5

- "The Extraordinary Ordinary: Seeing the Magnificence of God in the Ordinary, Volume 1"

- "If The Tears Are Real: A Fresh Look At the Death and Resurrection of Lazarus"

- "The Extraordinary Ordinary: Seeing the Magnificence of God in the Ordinary, Volume 2"

- "The Other Side: Finding Peace In Middle Of Your Storm"

Coming in 2026

- "The Extraordinary Ordinary: Seeing the Magnificence of God in the Ordinary, Volume 3

Follow Duke for future releases at https://dukestone.net/author

Made in the USA
Columbia, SC
20 January 2026

77837087R00094